T0016238

NORTH OF MIDDLE ISLAND

D.A. LOCKHART

KEGEDONCE PRESS, 2023

Copyright © by D.A. Lockhart.
July 2023

Published by Kegedonce Press
11 Park Road, Neyaashiinigmiing, ON N0H 2T0
Administration Office/Book Orders: P.O. Box 517, Owen Sound, ON N4K 5R1
www.kegedonce.com

Printed in Canada by Trico Packaging & Print Solutions
Managing editor: Kateri Akiwenzie-Damm
Art Direction: Kateri Akiwenzie-Damm
Design: Chantal Lalonde Design
Author's photo: D.A. Lockhart

Library and Archives Canada Cataloguing in Publication

Title: North of Middle Island / D.A. Lockhart.
Names: Lockhart, D. A., 1976- author.
Identifiers: Canadiana 20230473989 | ISBN 9781928120377 (softcover)
Classification: LCC PS8623.O295 N67 2023 | DDC C811/.6—dc23

All rights reserved. No part of this book may be reproduced in any form or by
any electronic or mechanical means including information storage and retrieval
systems, without permission in writing from the Publisher. Member of Access
Copyright Sales and Distribution – www.litdistco.ca

For Customer Service/Orders
Tel 1-800-591-6250 Fax 1-800-591-6251
100 Armstrong Ave. Georgetown, ON L7G 5S4
Email: orders@litdistco.ca

We acknowledge the support of the Canada Council for the Arts which last year
invested $20.1 million in writing and publishing throughout Canada.

 Canada Council Conseil des arts
for the Arts du Canada

We would like to acknowledge funding support from the Ontario Arts Council,
an agency of the Government of Ontario.

 ONTARIO ARTS COUNCIL
CONSEIL DES ARTS DE L'ONTARIO
an Ontario government agency
un organisme du gouvernement de l'Ontario

For Eleanor and Grey-Grey

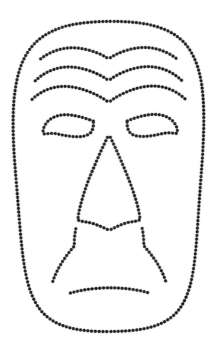

CONTENTS

Ktàpihëna

KTÀPIHËNA

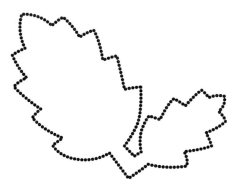

Measurements

Our great southern nation
has proclaimed the northern
to be two feet higher
and the border runs through
      the Neutral Sea. That

we lose twenty meters of gravel
      to a flood measured
in years rather than fronts.

      We live in fear
          of measurement
      how it can be layered
      upon the earth we walk.

      The lake will be more green
          than the earth where Zug
      meets Rouge. We measure
      fear by clear mornings.

      Tëmakwe was spotted
          at the north end,
          beneath a slouching lighthouse.

      Monarchs arrive
      like dogwood pollen.

      Pelicans have begun to eat
          gaagaagiishibag.

When the ferry arrives
between windstorms
      and government austerity,
      we are certain
          that the measure
      of water
between Westview and Kingsville
is counted
      by light reflected
in the mirroring
      of all too human distance.

North of Middle Island

Isolation is a measure
of knowing the distance
to places others call home.

Amidst the summits
that were drowned
by the warming rage
of a great atavistic bear
this isolation spreads
out in the turquoise
of our Neutral Sea.

mënatay one rests upon.
mënatay one must become.

North of Middle
Island there is only us,
standing here inches
above the lake.

Shukëlimënatay,
we watch from shore
the bruise blue outline
of what has always
been hoped to be
another mënatay
believe in our measures.

Rooster Tail Grand Entrance North on Victoria

Another rooster tail
           gravel   road
           storm front
           peters out   into   August
blue sky dryness.

Dust in fluid motion,
           cast-off by a
           minivan as it
plies northward.

Dryness we know is seasonal.

Rise and fall of unsettled
dislodged earth
        frames a grand entrance
        for each visitor.

        A full-on strut
        of arms
        of legs
        of cocked-up heads,
        chikënëm
        in mid-stride

crossing Victoria,
        from soy bean patches
        to poplar wind breaks

        each shifting
        kicks-up dirt

        a claim

on something that cannot be owned.

Let it lie,

this kicked up earth,
                                        descended,
                                        resting on
                ground
between   determined fractures
            of green.

In between

all of us, clay
            upon Thomas McKee's
limestone footprint.

All of us, kicking
            dirt skyward
as we arrive to new places
                                like this.

The hand full of full-time islanders know
that the ferry runs full,
five times daily, and it is far
better to watch that boat
leave from the stone wall
piled against a battered shore
than to come again to places
            you know little of
            and sprinkle so quickly
            with what little earth
            is willing to give.

Dull Thuds over Waabiishkiigo Gchigami

Inland, on this three-part island, let it
resonate. Through summer night darkness
these dull, distant thunderbirds claps are

reminders rolling off stirred-up lake-effect spirits
that even distant storms find their ways to glacial
land upturned and shallow. Steady as nightfall

come to this limestone gouge, torrential
skies cloaking distant portions of Neutral Sea
inland, in this farmhouse, we may doubt glacial

ancestors in this bathtub sea, this night sky free
of the pathways left by stars, redolent grandmother
of a moon. The fear of trying one with the sea.

Here rattles a middle island farmer soul. Other
than fear or love he wanders between rooms
of this farmhouse, coaxed by light of grandmother.

Outside, clouds are broken and light casts
long blooms of saturated òxehëmu and we
watch on this three-part island. Listen well,
to these dull, distant claps of thunderbirds.

Kwèn'shùkwënay Dwell Beneath

We have seen, from Fish Point,
the creature of shallows and shoals
rising, writhing, against lake currents,
a tide onto itself. Kwèn'shùkwënay
dwell beneath us as they always have
and rise to greet those along shore
forgetful of what stirs beneath. Know
that we have seen these defenders
of copper as they lie in wait, bristle
at the passing touch of the air above,
in patience to render forth sharp tail,
body part feline, part snake, break
the horizon of lake water, overpower
with hungry jaws and crash down upon
that which must be cast to the bottom
of this shallow sea. Time between
falling leaves and first snow they stir
from sunshine hibernation, remind us
that the waters between the turtle shells
we walk upon know a creation beyond
words like Erie, sovereignty, and myth.

Alex Lifeson Doesn't Play Flying Vs

Know that flying V guitars
are all for show. Nothing in
them practical for the act
of coaxing song from hands.

> Cooking sun off port deck
> bench tops and the loose-legged
> 10 am hangover sunglass glare.

Music is forty percent show
the rest a lament for scenes
recalled from vague memories
boasted about on ferry crossings

> Cormorants stream by in an exact
> Dave Mustaine V, blue edge cutting
> atop the stillness of the Neutral Sea.

There is always Rush; the shows
one should have and did not see.
Music is heritage passed between
tavern bards and amateur sound guys.

> Sun bears down on outstretch
> black jeans, hands that knows beer
> cups better than paper cup lattes.

Know that Lifeson didn't play
a Flying V for Rush. What it comes
down to is show as much as music.
One lives for music. Arrives for show.

> Sunglasses dipped low, eyes caress
> bronzed legs of two brunette mainlanders,
> island bound, laughing at shared secrets.

He only played telecasters to empty
rooms. Confesses college radio loved
him and proclaims the show to be king
and 2112 to be the palace he didn't enter.

Clinging to Dry Earth at Henry's Marsh

Azaadi fluff tumbles on wind
headed by return of midday sun,
the air, in unwavering density,
above a sun-cooked marsh, coats
browned grasses, rests against fallen
trunks and branches. This desiccate
road is hard under foot, tooth-rattle
discomfort of a reminder that bedrock
above water determines that rain shall
not fall here. Yet, azaadiwag descend,
seeking ground through ordained
motions. Our world is this dirt road
between lake and still water marsh
and it lies covered in the gossamer
of future generations grown tired
of surging winds, blanching sun.
Ground half held by exhaustion
half in stubbornness and half in
the belief that forgetful, fickle
creation can be survived if only one
finds hard ground to rest upon.

These Fields Inland Carry a Frustration

Before these fields, recurring gouges
of dried out marsh, declare from atop
this weathered porch, "you sons of bitches."

Proclaim that creation is stubborn in
its resistance to "rational" order. It lies
stagnant in reflection of lost malarial marshes

This reclaimed Tuwèhtuwe land unflinching
in its drive to be that which absentee
industrial farming demands that it be.

Listen: bellflowers in the wind, the taunts
of killdeers and barn swallows call
backs to the way the land wishes to be.

Before you, everything from horizon
to horizon is left to rise in middle lake
sun, shimmer in passing winds.

Crosschannel pumps draw subsurface
Water into tree-fenced ditches, making
three islands into one, and you at centre.

Consider that which follows, knowing
that water understands only one course
and that beans, corn, and wheat are covers
that capitalists shroud how creation embraces
us and fields of land frustrate the hungry
and thirsty that toil to pull money from dry dirt.

The Room Upstairs

From above,
       in the heat of a slow-cooked
       bedroom, the ancestors
       are closer. Wind
coming in hard
       the wrong way,   pushes clouds
and lightning away from us,
          to Kingsville
maybe Harrow.

       Even the electric insects
have fallen into slumber,
       calmed by passing
          feu follet
       in the fallow bean field
       to wet timber bon-fire
constructed in vain hopes
       to punish absent punkwsàk
       that sought portions of us
       in this night without grandmother.

Up here,
       living feels impossible;
       tall grass waves
       along the fallow fields,
undeniable the shadow
       and five-story
          wind
          breaks
punctuate in the dying light
of the spirit cast-off
from the white path above us.

Mechanical,
       the drone and motion
       of tabletop fan
       sings me to sleep
as the kisses of distant electric storms
trace dream paths
       through the darkest of nights.

Ghosts of Cranes

Frosted grey-green
    like beach glass
    uncovered by a
    tahkokën tempest,

our Neutral Sea foments
    even sky
with writhing body
        visible
in the breaches
    of white
    violence below.

The distance   between   lake bottom
                                          and sky
    is shallowest here,
without sand,
    and the flaking rock
        gives way
to fossils and loose gravel.

This is land's end,
    the final steps before
    a northern country
    crumbles
    into
    the
    fickle waters beyond.

Tread lightly here.
    Lightly,
    like a beach-shuffling tern,
    talons raking sand
    like a breath.

Know the petrified past
    flakes away
    to grit,
    covers creation.

Through the settled dust,
    consider Maumee mùxula,
    cutting the impossible gap
        between
    shore and Middle Island's shadow.
    Our crane relations, sublimated
to dust and wave residue,
    apparitions that refuse
    to leave or stay.

Thunder Spirits Make Gentle Chëmàmës Road

Oh, tower above this all,
    collected bird song
        and dust kicked up by
        chëmàmsàk as they dance
from ditch   to   ditch.
    Rise to greet
    Kishux as she burns above
    alvar, vine-wrapt dead tree
    trunks, swaying Queen Anne's lace.

Tame this spinning head.

Take these gifts.

Roll. Cook. Rise in the dew-point
    of day-promised rain,
    of an island fueled
on the redemptive native
    of shore
    in an expansive sea of islands

Divided sky
    against
        this July
        haze
wind-blown high,
    from here ashuwixën
    rises and I clear
this spot of alvar
    for a lodge
    part treaty
    part romance.

Gustave Fulfills the Prophecies at the Victoria Road Workshed
for Gustave Morin

We are enveloped
        in electricity
of distant storms
        separated
by glacial limestone grooves,
spun in heated updrafts.

From inside,
        we are witness

to how water suspends
        its downward drive
to avoid this island.

Gustave, at fluorescent centre
        of this workshed,
                surrounded
        in farm parts
            from the last generation,
            swings
    at   the super cluster of mayflies,
            with flailing hands

illustrates how one kicks
back at the dry side
        of bug hatches.

        A tightly rolled
        joint mimics
        the motions
        of a vengeful Jehovah
        walking into Cairo,
        dipping in and out
        of the shadows,
        proclaims that fame
        is measured by how others
        don't understand you.

His words trail
    into this crackling
        darkness,
        orange like waves
    of sea buckthorn branches,

    his speech carried
        on the backs
        of thousands of troubled
        mayflies, as they recoil
        into the night.

Collecting Tipi Poles from the Pelee Island Transportation Company

for William Dwyer

Understand they are lodgepole,
all seventeen of them, kuwehòki
imported to this Carolinian island
from a stand outside the federal
prison at Deer Lodge, Montana.
These are the ribs that must hold
canvas against sky. We collect
them beside the warehouse at
the federal dock. Between arrivals
and summer storms we pull in
and load them atop a sputtering
Subaru. Two Indians moving ribs
of high plains housing design
onto land that has been forgetful
of its Indigenous past. This ringing
early summer heat, still left over,
from too many house beers with
the ferry crew, and tavern talk
about visiting wrestlers, the tales
they leave in their wake, truth
and fiction, our past lingers like
the humidity of last night's storm.

The transport is simple enough,
slow across the island's one paved
road, the collection is what matters.
Done at speed, far too late into
the day, and with an unearned
confidence of two urban naxans
figuring out how to add a touch
of themselves to this stolen land.

Swallows Run Frantic at Water's Edge

Trace the pathways
of swallows, running
veins atop Waabiishkiigo,
criss-crossing whirlpools
left by minnows,
        stalking the same hatch.

Discarded, yellow ash leaves
islands unto themselves
crest and fall on this lake
swollen past temperament
by distant snowfalls,
        creation rising to meet creation

Beyond us, northward
our land peters out into
shipping lanes, currents
of sand, algae, driftwood.
Each caress of this lake
        refreshes us, shows us

Horizon holds mid-lake
lighthouse, toilet shaped,
blotting out Wheatley beyond.
A lesson that lake freighters,
pleasure boat fishermen,
        ignore in due course.

The lake, creation moves
slow. Swallows frantic atop
it, us lazy on this beach,
and the water rises, another
freighter steams past lighthouse
        green moves atop high waves.

Ode to Sea Buckthorn

Bleaching late morning
sunlight fails to diminish
the brilliance of your orange
berries. Shine on, plastic
and hopeful like debris,
flotsam bobbing by Scudder
after a nipën squall, foreign,
distinguished from slate
of sky traumatized water,
an arrival, potentially useful.
We become chkënakw,
hungry for their colour
vivid through thicket
smooth as smoggy glare
of our Midwestern sun
upon your transplanted
Mediterranean flesh.
Sins can be forgiven
with enough sugar. Chalk
of your crushed berries
holds the tang, powdery
sweet of childhood birthday
parties, ersatz yet comforting
juice, and a sweet that lingers
dry on your tongue. In a place
where one celebrates what
stays rather than what came
first, believe that no better
arrival holds tighter to these
islanders' lips that crushed
berries and your earthen
sweetness of one who
survived storms, waves,
passages, unlikely rooting.

Phantoms of Three Islands at the Edges of Ruggles Run

Across the gravel
          and dust line
that transects
          the middle portion
          of this collective island,
stitches pheasant farms volunteer fire hangars
abandoned homesteads single shack airfields,
we are the needle
          and thread
pulling three islands
          into one.

Daylight falling
          into brilliance of creation
     through prism
          of gathering clouds, we cut
     north, gaze latched
     on canal-side tree
     line for egrets
     and wetënteis,

          fellow refugees

from waters thought of as mainland
industrial dumping grounds,
a churning green inland sea
     overcome
     by the disappearance
     of the Great Black Swamp.

Every revolution
     of tire
     and wheel,
                    we cut
     back to a dried marsh
     bottom farmhouse, our search
of darkening soybean fields
for a half-used road is secondary

to the visions we seek in trees
huddled against still inland water.

Three appear.
        Tëmakwe amble away
        from headlights in the distance.
Amble canal side, apparitions
        of islands before Scudder.
Sky the colours of wetënteis
        underbelly, stretched
        out like a hundred million
ancestors returning here,
to this Creation's medicinal centre,
        that point where Lasalle
        can be undone
        and the sing-song
        of Anishinaabemowin
        can carry through cedar
        and ash windbreaks.

We are urged on
        to destination
        by bisecting flight paths
        of Kildeers and distant
        light of a farmhouse
holding to the earth beneath it all.

Pishkok Perform Sunset Ceremony Feast

The windbreaks to our south
are poplars dipped in ink,
left to dry beneath the bruised
edges of twilight. Through a thin
band of retreating light, erratic
pitch and yawl of pishkok wings
shuffle the air between alànkòk
that burn into our emerging night.
Forgotten connections between
them, these distant glimmers
of ancestors. Long stilled after
the skeleton dance, growing
fewer in time's passage. Pishkok
feigning their motion among
the growing darkness. Drone
electric from mufflehead swarms
meets throaty boom of feeding
hawks frantic to snap up
what remains. We sit along this
field, listening rather than watching
the approaching night. Ancestors
igniting in diminishing numbers
above us, and our dancers hardly
visible, still vocal, feast away as
the light bleeds into and is replaced
by a dull glare of city lights on
the horizon. Awash in a deepening
bruise of our waking long slide
towards morning and beyond,
I understand that at the edges
we may witness portions of our world
taken from us, however diminished,
but the quiet stunted darkness
beyond will not return what is lost.

Achimëwakàn of a Pumphouse

after Wallace Stevens

They placed this pumphouse
along the island's eastern shore.
It made this slovenly wetland
surround us like a lake couldn't.

All the ways that a simple shed
can dominate creation around it,
more than a jar, more than a flag,
more than a clearcut forest, here
the domination is more mundane.

Dry land behind us, still water
canals gouged well below water
line idle beside and Kildeers sing
out to the fields, to the wind breaks,
to the crusty gravel road shoulders,
each note over fallow fields, each
not a misplaced sun-warmed kiss.
And the cormorants and gulls circle
the sky and heave of water before
us. And the pumphouse still, took
dominion everywhere water dare
not touch, cast out what came in.

Harvest

It goes through the night
like the call of barred owls,
screams of red foxes hunting
for future kin, the shuffle
of light and inland marsh
along dark roads, the weight
of a season's sun contained
in the caravan full of what
it takes to get by on this island.

And the normal is a patrol,
and migration, on an island
reserved for passing through.
When one discovers their pieces
of creation, they dig deep, are
tethered to the earth they rattle
with steel, with blade, with their
light's leading edge in the closing
hours of another autumn.

Sparks that Shall Not Ignite

Rise by morning
to the crackle
of American hunters
shooting at freedom
on an island they
don't own. Sparks

of distant violences,
behaviours not readily
forgotten, carried
in RNA strands.
We are amalgamations
of bacteria, viruses,

stored in flesh cages
though an existence
measured by time,
how we pass it. And
the shots crackle
across soybean fields

threaten like fires that
shall not ignite. Crackle
as they might, here
is not their land, here
the day will burn on
and the kildeers will

swoop across orange
dirt roads between us.

Ode to Hamm's Baloney Sandwich

Through you, I believe
this island holds
its Indigenous soul.
Thick cut, meat slurry
            rich enough to be
a white's man rez
lusting after fresh water
resting at our lake's centre.

While you left
We've come past
            the retreating light
            blamed on high
            lake levels, green
            sludge from Ohio.

This corner store
            cum beachcomber
            dive bar plays
            the funeral pyre
            to lost decades.

We are here to eat.

Just us. The shell of a bar
on the quiet side of an era
on this island between nations.

And we've arrived
            for Indian steak
                        in a white man's bar.

Server, sits beneath
middle-aged man portrait
            speaks into empty room
            as if she knows
                        it will not fill again.

Screaming at Foxes Above Fish Point

We drive through the island
thick night, between darkness
that we cut at right angles,
with our car along gravel roads,
and we scathe the shadows
for foxes, crystalline eye flare
in the shadows beyond
our knives' edge. We search
until we collide with land's end.
Erie restless against shore,
we stop and scream our cries
into unrelenting, darkness
as it rises from lake swells
meeting land's rocky edge.

èlikhatink

The inward path
     is patchy, narrow
     into fresh lung
     air of a forest
     beyond solitary
     road's edge.

Through poison ivy,
     thistle,
       swampy milkweed.
     inward.

Believe the sun
     arrived
     as needed
     that autumn
     is not
     yet here.

we walk

on water, as if blessed
     by ancestral water walkers
     as if their essence
     arises
     from thin alvar soils
     beneath
     us

toes pushed to cold mud,
     find successive roots
     binding it all

to this island. And we follow
     this
     path
     inward

clean

through still
     falling
          leaves

to a new encampment,
     a new season.

Henderson Road Slow Roll

Darkness is the essence
        cleaved by headlights.
We know this is at the heart
of this night drive. Slow
over dirt-roads, slow
over recent-storm washouts,
we are the hunters, we
are that which stalks
between cascading leaves.
through thickening
autumn air, we roll slow,
eyes fixed to perimeter,
hopeful, searching for
radiant eyes in tall grass.

we   slow   roll   through
        bird reserve,
                pheasant farm,
bike paths,   shuttered cottages

And cattails weave
        in cleaving lights

and we are left wanting
        and drifting onward, slowly.

Pòkhakeho

Even here, where earth
does not rise much above
high water crests, the dead
haunt us. Our past is a burial
mound, our present the grass
atop the rise of land. Clufton's
Y at Harris Garno overlooks
the island's active quarry.
The newcomers have dug
down, tempting the lake
beyond, hauling up the past
for roadways, foundations.

Here these mounds are used
to hold back the lake, water,
what wishes to return home.
What is natural, what is new
is more difficult to tell from
what is necessary. Grey dust
and loose gravel by the fence
demarks the wound's edges.
And from here, the land
rises sharply in the distance
where to the road meets
the western dyke, fallow fields
and scrub brush wash the
distant between.

Waabiishkiigo Gchigami Stills Herself in the Presence of the Pelee Islander II

She stills herself, body like Erie
Street cement, punctuated by ridges,
ripples of the tension cast by wind
patterns. Know that resting gulls shall
be tossed in the fury that must follow.
Now they bob languid in surface eddies
of a loading ferry, this steadying
of evening performed by new monarch
as she floats dockside. At rest before
the last mainland run of this ending day
from this island, both lake and boat
are indifferent to three passing bikers,
I want them to make note of those
choosing to leave before another week
sets in. Survivors are those that weather
a still lake, a nasty northwestern clipper,
the steady rise of lake waters. We live
our lives as if this stillness that proceeds
departures is the world each of us shares.
Yet, we live in between. Know the Neutral
Sea reflects a white and two-tone blue hull
with gold foil windows that is the boat
of consequence here at the edge of a nation.
Subtle, rippled, a near mirror to the world
above our sea hints nothing of lake bottom
littered with shipwrecks and front over
Michigan that shall unleash a poorer fate
for the gulls that bob leisurely in the space
between closing car deck and concrete dock.

Nearing Capone's Docks

The immediate sound is gravel
          as it pings out from tires,
casting rocks from the centre
close to the ditch,
          touching weeds.

Kawënshuwik, winakok sway
          in wind
          that courses
          upward
          towards lurking   mòchipwis
                    heat
                                        vents.
The lake beyond,
          obscured
          by trees,
          murmurs at
          shore rocks.

This is the quiet side of our island.
Where vision when it meets water
line, looks towards the Americans
                              beyond.

Monarchs dance
          in more passive air
          neared the roadtop
          and as we round
          the dog leg
          on this strange
          loyalist outpost,
          far from Dominion lands
          Neil Young bellers
          Cowgirl in the Sand,
          into an adjacent marshland
          filled with century old pier
          boards and dock
                    posts.

We slow to a standstill,
      holding like an egret
            before flight,
      buffeted
      by recursive
      wind gusts.
and overlook
      the abandoned
      docks,
      where two life-times ago,
      a murderous
      liquor smuggler
      found
      temporary peace.

Witnessed the lake
roll between here
and where he pulled
money from others.
Perhaps smoked a cigar
we still can't afford
and thought mostly
about leaving here.

And still this lake
      rolls beyond
      the crumbling
      breakers, refuses
      to enter this still
      water and address
      the slow rot
      of a port built
      by bootlegging
      and murder.

Crystal Caves

Ashore, we have heard
of spontaneous growth,
a lake reaching to sky,
water rising in winter
sun, Spirit Moon night.

Chicken Islands Reef
pulling ice heavenwards,
heaving crystalized waves
atop crystalized waves. Us
ashore, thinning ice between.

We understand Creation
has beauty we shall never
touch. Known only through
traces brought to us by
migrating water fowl.

We stand here, west facing,
eyes to the horizon between
the Chicken Islands, searching
for distant myths, believing we
see crystallized folds on the horizon.

Piskewëni and a Darkness Wrought Through 2112

At lake's centre,
    piskewëni comes
    on slow, stubborn.

Akin to heat leaving
    rock at two AM,
    its departure,
like a slow goodbye,
    as both ground
        and sky
  learn to merge in
Carolinian shadow.

I traverse
  the darkness
    in this hallow body
    of a refurbished Subaru,

    out long past
        when awènik walk
        this island.

it is better to dream
    than face the darkness.

Geddy cries into the night,
    howling lost guitar riffs

Under this cataclysmic epoch,
only the most tepid rocks surround
an intensifying night.

Survival at lake's centre,
after the brightest lights
have been extinguished
and all that remains

is the cautious hesitation
of engine clicks, rattles,
a soundtrack for this uptake
of another uncertain act
of survival.

At Centre Dyke road, the gravel ricochets
            to the hardest parts of the song.
And south, south I run
away from the eerie hue
of distant greenhouses
and towards the degrees
            of darkness cast
            by our nearby
            rust-belt neighbours.

Our Slow Decomposition in the Reflection of Perry's Victory Monument Near the Shore of Middle Bass Island

Perhaps the line begins
where Perry's Victory
Monument dissipates
in the waves, reflecting
still summer mornings.

Hangover of last night,
its celebratory lights,
robust Foreigner tracks,
the sluggishness lingers,
prodded by gull cries.

And the bob of Erie,
beneath, touching bottom
curling upward, outward.
Lines still not visible,
Perry's statue unseen.

Here all the waters touch
the Midwest beyond.
What we touch becomes
us, the gentle bob on
surface belies a graveyard
of settler ships below.

Here it is all water, what
it touches, it takes, holds,
blends horizon to sky,
mirages of mountains,
ghost ships and you, eyes
bleary against early haze
witness it all wash away.

Decomposition is slow,
tireless, and cut raw
by the torment of gulls

hunting for vanishing fish.
Borders, monuments, our
fleeting passage here lost
in the bobbing waters
that touch bottom, reach
for the morning fresh sky.

PIPER*

*A rarely true folktale. First told by JW at the Moraviantown Big House ceremony November 1998. Transcribed here by the poet into familiar poetic form.

Canto Kwëti:

Listen, with oiled wings   outstretched in heat
of shore line rocks   seen reflected in sheen
rich feathers wind   rocked how they defy
shoreline air, bring   forth a slipstream heard
thirteen heavens above.   Oh, that creator awakens
namèsàk deep beneath,   that they shall stir,
school in collected   currents, search out
stones of past storms   bring them to surface.
Unfurl visions, history   the you shall visit
through these words myth,   past wind to life.
That I shall find   the rhythmic slipstream
and lead from wing   tips, lifted from lake
shore above poplar   stands into airy eddies
swirling above dirt   roads, vineyards, dust
rooster tails cast by   seasonal tourist motion.
Each displaced grain   thrown skyward, earth
bound, but reaching   for what rests above.
Settle among us,   words akin to dust,
and sprout story,   recall what has passed.
Pour forth as witness   to the gifts of creator
that a poet, faithful   to stones carried
from lake bottom   by ancestral fish,
build a fresh earth   upon which to rest,
and recount origins   of good, evil, and how
this southern island   has long been home
to both, yet once   was delivered from evil.
Be that this poet,   breathes flame to lives
lived, restore myth   to being, memory
ignited, and burns   like sun atop Neutral
Sea. In this tavern   westward eyes fixed
on crooked path.   That these words stir
the spirit of Piper   beyond these shores,
saturate this parched   air of oft-shunned
earth, awash in fickle   lake waves, a halcyon
home to awènik,   austere, hewn near
from the soft edges   of grand nations.

Roderick George Toombs,   risen from prairie soil,
billed as Glaswegian,   born to open roads,
whistlestop companies,   working class taverns.
Minneapolis jobber,   Manitoba heel,
road dog everyman,   revenger of Solie.
Of quick-tempered   rail cop lineage,
let us hear of   him how circumstance
makes ahinu from   the common man,
how foundations of   place are forgotten
in the breaks between   seasons. Let us recall.
the surety of his   strut into the ring,
through dirty backlots,   fleabag taverns, arenas.
In his might, one   name from his six,
Rowdy Roddy Piper is   referred to as Piper.

This one island   made of three, once
heated in a temper   of Tuwèhtuweyok
inland camp fires,   flowered in honour songs
of island hopping   and successful hunts,
joy in reaching of   furthest regions of
ancestral homelands.   Unspoken history
of how one's spirit   mingles with one's land,
rejects the namings   forced upon it by
greedy newcomers,   allows those that walk
with it to share   spirit, become
reflections of one   another, enter into
naxkùntëwakàn.   Naturally, this is
the state of all   things. Paths shared,
in words, in deeds,   in what is taken
in what is given.   This one island
that we call Pelee   upheld in peace
between swells of   a fickle Neutral Sea.

Two generations here   Hamm presided over,
this island, through   spirit, through deed,
through north shore   tavern, an open door
to those that walked   the island's gravel ways.
Illness descended,   like green algae slurry
coating of the shore   washed in from a dying
bay at that mouth   of a distant river named

for keepers of our   ancestral inland fires.
Illness that choked   breath from Hamm
as pitay broke life   from our Opeksipu
homelands, broke   spirit and lives
from our Unami   ancestors. As Neolin
warned: an epidemic   of epic settler hunger
would and did press   life from our world,
leave open wounds   forced us to walk
across a continent   with our ancestors'
bones, build treaty   trailed by hunters.
We were warned   of wicked medicine
and understood that   evil can take root
in all places, sacred   and profane. Death
is a side effect of   evil medicines arriving.

And so, it passed   that Scudder lost
their nikanixink,   a grand natural man
of cheap libations,   one who lead by
act, by joy, by   every jovial move.
Isaac Hamm had fought an invisible foe
fought well, but   was overcome from
within. An illness   that ate insidious
like pitay on shore,   squeezed from within.
When Hamm's spirit   passed from sandy
northside shores to   the White Way we
one day will all   walk, òkwsàk cried
out from scattered woods,   southside
vineyards, backyard   firepits. Bellered
sadness and guided   his slipstream soul
from his island   along the Gchi-Ojiig's way.
As those loud howls,   hung above the lake,
the greenhouse lights   of Leamington gutted
the path of stars,   signaled a tear in
the world, told evil   where to land, take
root. And for seven   nights, lights seared
the sky, calling out   after òkwsàk returned
to silent lingering   along gravel lanes
and wind breaks.   On the eighth night
lights diminished   and dry heaving
clouds crowded in.   Sapëlehële cracking

dry through ominous   banks of dirty clouds,
unsettled copper   protectors, unseen
had gathered below   pulled remains
from ship burial   grounds at bottom
of our Neutral Sea.   Sapëlehële gathered
above this island,   lurking, inspected
quiet dark waters,   departed before calm
of daybreak. Island   wreathed in dull light,
stilled with grief,   steady herself as if
stitched back together   by shifting migrations
of cormorants, gulls,   killdeers. Defiant in
steady braidings,   sewn back together.
Islanders continued   quotidian concerns
despite their grief,   in spite of dreadful
ominous signs, seas   still against shore,
chëmàmsàk lazy   in their Cooper's
Road foraging,   firecrackers gone
quiet in vineyards.   Virulent mourning
among those Hamm   left behind, alarmed
township leaders.   They lifted their
bodies to motion   hearts bent to ground
they continued on   in a coma of grief.
Became an island-wide   illness, that wore
on from day to   night back to day.

On the tenth day   tired of somber
atmosphere, unclear   futures, unlikely past,
Vintner Guido   gathered with elders
in the shed behind   the shell of the old
Casino at land's   end. Electric carnival
of distant Sandusky   sprinkled the horizon
an alien mainland   through maple stands
shadows huddled   along the shore, spoke
of past and future   of island life forever
changed. And lights   across the lake, neon
refractive, out   of time with residents,
with our dry land,   they danced in loops,
cavorted to sky   in shafts of burning
blues and raucous   crimsons, racing
towards sky then   water, tumbling

between worlds   of waking and beyond.
Each rise and fall   steeped full with
uncertainty of this   island's unfolding
present. Horizon   ablaze, hovering
as a muted spectre.   Specific need
for testimony   delivered to
and between those   left behind. Guido
gathered them all,   ten in total,
and with well-aged   wine served warm
in dim lantern light,   open door to lake,
they spoke of stories   brought to their secluded
home and mixed like   myth coaxed, borrowed
out of vacuous necessity,   filled their island niche
of history with tales   outside their home.

Ambrose, island bird   man, boldly recounted
old Tuwèhtuweyok   tales of water serpents,
clouds of amimiyòk,   appetite of mainlanders
for brief stints in   their bucolic island home.
Their hunger clear   in lake-side cottages
used for two months   a year, monsters on
edges for a hollowing   out homestead of hearty
survivalists. Serenity   comes from strength,
out-lasting the whims   of come-from-aways,
caring for stretches   of creation gifted
to you and yours.   Youth is foreign
to this island, he   intones through
nostalgic tales of   ethereal twilight skies
bespeckled with   sparkler pedals
and laughter,   languid walks along
beach and gravel   roads, broad enough
between poplars and   sycamores, parading
wants and memory   aside each other.
This beautiful island   bathed in Neutral Sea,
not fragile, lethargic   and likely to witness
tales beyond the cranes   and supernatural serpents.
Ominous signs linger   amongst salamanders,
kildeers are on edge,   and beavers thicken
the walls of their den   against coming storms.

Ivan spoke wistful   of Sunday wrestling
matches, witnessed   through white fuzz
of Toledo broadcast   television, a sacred
service of powerful   men, violence-prone
encounters of good   and evil, heels, heroes.
Working class gospels   for folks that Christian
proclamations failed,   feigned selflessness
of collection baskets,   Oldsmobile charity
for priests, genocidal   preachings, actions
against peoples   who remained present
on lands claimed   by their god, a lesser
one without strength   in suplexes, no-holds-
barred cage matches,   marker-drawn signs
raining praise. This   is the people's religion.
Priests had visited here,   ventured ashore solely
for professions' sake.   They stayed mere hours,
islanders knew they,   as nearly everyone
else, took both money   and means to their
large homes made across   the water. Most islanders
gathered before their   televisions, back glow
immersions of their   true priests, immaculate
reception of Hogan leg   drops upon a giant,
In full vida-chrome   colour, they gathered
when ferry or plane   failed to arrive. Island
theirs, free to choose   the path they follow,
they attended myth,   experienced abundant joy,
understood salvation   enters sauntering down
the alley to the ring.   Resonating bells calling
spectacle to begin,   declaring service has
concluded, separating   warriors, signaling
victors from those   vanquished, promising
decisiveness in simple   sweet declarative tones.

Ivan declares Pelee   an island of other
sacredness, drawn   from steady creation,
mirrored in Sunday   services of cold-cut
sandwiches, beers,   and belt defenses
from Goliathan   men in packed game
halls, foreign legions,   Masonic ballrooms,
occasional ice barns,   iconographies of those

that lived and have   lost by their labour.
If faith were to   rescue them from
their deep existential   gloom, let it draw
from grand men,   good and evil who
bleed for others' joy,   relish their ornate
adornment, move   attuned to hype
music walks-ins, staged   pyrotechnic mayhem.
Left alone, amidst   a vast lake, spirit
finds sacredness in   the familiar, secures
belief in simple   benign childish acts.

Irma speaks of visions   of sensual gold, visiting
here from afar, valleys,   mountain vistas, ocean
breezes caressing   congested freeways.
Upon surging winds   of oceanic western
origins, two shall   arrive by dark sky.
He shall shimmer,   shine as ancestors
in still lake reflection   of a patient surface,
a mirror of creation   around, backwards
replicas of the things   they appear to be.
He is called in name   Nkuli Punkw, his
movements certain   as xkuk before he
strikes, slithering   skin as he rubs
creation, a sensual   joy, a craving of his
that fills around him   all to smothering.
Flaxen hair, beefcake   bulging muscles,
obsidian spandex   and sparkling metallic
face paint to coax   kwèn'shùkwënay
to surface, he strides   in a reflective spectacle.
She, his binary, cigar   belching smoke, form
fitting dress, elegant   as ahtuwok following
forest shadows at dusk.   Sheer clung feminine
power seen in outline   of muscular frame
beneath encouraging   evening wear, known
as Marlena, wicheochi   to Nkuli Punkw, wit
to balance, strength   to brawn, she to him
as land to water, calm   to storm, love to lust.
These two shall arrive   like shattered dreams,
a twenty-four karat   production, chaos
in glitter-bomb style.   Blow-ins bent upon

covering their island   in unfamiliar coveting
dust, spectacular alien   defilement, smothering
and all-encompassing   this shall be their arrival
to this land edging   two nations, oft lorn.
They come for wine,   for pheasant, coronal
sunsets, quiet that   one surmises comes
through quiet control,   through domination,
and has left only   the usurpers' legacy
on land garnered   by lasting violence.

Kelly rises, circles   the fire ring in steps,
counts back her   uncertainty of a future
in completed rounds.   Resonance of foot falls
felt in contortions   of firm, giving earth
beneath them. Thuds   like dulled drums,
a stirring of spirit   beneath, not shaking
but vibrating. Hope   in repetition, heroes
can arrive, dragged ashore   like Ahkonachimu,
those least likely   to liberate and leave.
What of warriors,   heroes from a world
beyond their ring of   coastal sand and rock?
Shall their story be   of endings, of shame
from standing last,   inept at survival,
bystander at the fall,   before one's fine days,
and the earth beneath   erodes all their traces.
Irma's words broach   an end beyond Hamm,
true as her dreams   of deep algae mats,
smothered break walls,   bleak foretelling's of
many of their island's   multitude of calamities.

Visions are warnings,   variations of probability,
gifts from the Creator,   this Guido reminds them.
With warnings come   hope, way finders for
likely turns, blessed   time to see them arrive.
For Irma's vision   contains a verifiable
goodness, that with   it the unseen way
lit by a possible hero   that limits bad visions
to passing nightmares,   phases to move through.
Hamm arrived this   way, how he hobbled
old Man McCormick,   that thieving oligarch,

liberated the island
and sweet yacht rock.
into Erie's cold waves
and a true arsenal of
Before Irma, seers,
foretold of good
that would chase evil
They arrive from afar
bring with them lives
from. Habits, morals
acts, allows a claim

through libations
Sent the old monster
with Asia, Chilliwack,
rock vinyl and tapes.
born of lost lineage
fighters such as Prince
back into the waters.
like all people here,
meant to run away
that foment future
at chitaninu by action.

Ivan recounts Piper
on highland bagpipe
like the Essex Regiment.
vision-like testimony.
his clan-less tartan
How it leads, follows
Dust cannot settle on
motion, from The Pas
to Atlanta and back
threatens our island,
to face this. Ivan
against lustful man
Oh, our salvation
tempered man of
good and bad, each
and given to move
heroes of creation
to the revolutions
in the need, joy
He has witnessed
on their holy day
many with golden-hair
practically lustful,
and in moments that
Sunday shall come
they shall all gather
and hold Toledo's
comes in wistful like

roaring to ringside
wails, broad stepping
He recalls him vivid
Knows of his trials,
of an everyman's kilt.
every leg-boot extension.
a creature in constant
to Portland, Billings
around again. Dust
and he knows how
saw his Fargo fight
and his lithe
lies in this short-
faults, made of decisions
came by honestly,
on as all such true
give themselves constant
of the world, revel
their niche provides.
Piper on WJLX
battle with huge men,
many driven, power hungry,
approaching overt lechery
are familiar, likely.
in six days, then
in Ivan's old garage
service as the ritual
lake fog in autumn,

soft between red   and bronze pulses of
distant maples, oaks,   and waters below. And
through the static, and   through well-worked cards
they shall know Piper   through his promos
through his entrance,   through rolling credits
and they shall follow   the path opened by
Irma's vision and   a lifetime of choosing
the proper gods   to spend sabbath with.
These ilaok are vain   like all ilaok tend
to be. Through praise   their paths shall meet.

Piskewëni draws   to numb glow dusk,
Carrianne leads them   in ceremony, gifts
of kwshatay, màxkw   pëmi, winkimakwsko,
added in song, in   smoky sweet embrace
of healing campfire.   Heavy, dense smoke
billowing out and   over the nearby shore.
Transplanted Unami,   she is tethered
to enough memory   and family lines to
call forth songs, ways,   the land feels true
to the earliest treaties   between awènik, earth,
all its inhabitants.   How to thank, how
to ask, how to call   the island a relation
rather than property.   This she explains
through her motions.   Thankful for the vision
hopeful that their ila   shall follow, that time
between arrivals shall   last no longer than
Kuhemena's cyclical   changes, empty to full.

Carrianne extinguishes   the bonfire, engulfing
flames in wet soil.   Fuming smoke, they leave
into the shadows.   There she stands alone
at land's end and   watches the lake dip
in recoiling light   of the land beyond
its sunken effigy   edging closer to shore,
Each ripple, Piskewëni   had come on rich,
deep as all thirteen   heavens dropped below.
Kelly sees a glimmer   grind against ripples,
a patina in the oil   sheen of the lake, aged
apprehends an island   belongs not to awènik

but to these waters,   what lurks beneath.
Simple fact that here,   a future is holding on.
Survival follows dual   paths cut deliberate by
ceremony and driven want   to war with invaders.

Canto Nisha:

Kuhemena reflects   crisp strips of light
atop lake surface,   little past her full
self, and her lustre   atop darkest waters
is sufficient to make   the star-poor sky
jealous, moody above   our island. Mëxumsa
Ehëliwsikakw stirred   by complaint, seethes
through the sky above,   stirs trees and lake
to frantic motion.   Prickly spine feeling
foretelling storms,   earth-shifting, in size
are inbound. First   on southern horizon
a golden light burns   to view, greets night
in its earliest state,   sweeps the distance
between shore, islands,   and the lake beyond.
In gathering darkness,   ghost light quickens
until metallic, reflects   rose gold sunset, born
to earth on Shattered   Dreams projections.
Twenty-four carat devil   creatures make arrival here,
descend Learjet steps   onto lonely taxi way,
a woman in long sheer   evening dress leads them
both, a block of a man   bearded in warrior
paint, following in trail   of rich Partagas smoke
spiraling from her cigar,   two arrivals strut between
their quieting jet and   blue cinder block garage
terminal for island arrivals.   Inside, Ivan greets them,
clears border crossings   with greenback bundle
and quick stamps, she   still burning cigar, speaks
with clan mother power,   settles paperwork like
chëlilhwès snatching fish   along the shoreline,
stout focus alongside   sharp motions, each
motion a reflective act   of her relentless hunt.

Ivan recognizes Nkuli   Punkw, replays old match
from Fargo, weeks back   versus King Flair. Bout
to take the Continental   Title. A high cathedral
service punctuated   with punishing attacks
from the ila before   him now. He won
that Sunday morning   service, with dramatic
monologues and bone   mauling crossbody

chops. He recalls this   man through violence
and yet he fears   the woman foremost.
Familiar, Ivan knows   his very form changed,
Nkuli Punkw arrives   preened in ceremonial
dress, he is carried   by directed purpose,
and clothed in gold   threaded hunting jacket,
silk feathered boa   and sheer black gloves
colour of a deadly   night lake. Rather than
speak he heaved,   he inhaled as a creature
taking in fresh land,   mind locked perpetually
in looming violence,   exhaled long heated
breaths that lay claim   to the corners touched,
that Fargo won belt   wrapped over his shoulder,
sways like the dead   skin of his prey.
Irma's vision had come   to be, two phantoms
made hyper real, passing   mundane a checkpoint
without flight plan,   without warning spare
a woman's vision.   They stood before Ivan.

He knew before she   spoke that what were
to follow were mere   markings on the path
determined by fate.   Ivan's duty to perform
questions he knew   answers to. Marlena
belching thick sweet   smoke, unveils customs
forms and purchase   agreements. She places
copies in Ivan's keeping   departs into the night,
Nkuli Punkw's glitter   dusted hair punctuates
their northern transit.   Ivan sees the shadows
greet them, engulfs   their edges. But glitter
trails off behind them   leaving dying blemishes
of light in the slate   of perfect shadow left.
He gathers the papers   and feels gentle softness
to them, shuffles them.   Ahtuhwixèkën shakes
free, covers the desk   forms a path to doors.

He reads over papers   long after pishkok take
to their pishkèk hunt   above the vineyards.
He finds visas paid   for, agreements forged
between mainland   banks, material wealth
of their deceased   nikanixink, his debts

carried forward then   cleared for fractions
of their cost, vision   creatures the purchasers
consuming, digesting   the carrion of a relation.
Days follow and Hamm's   Tavern's fate dawns
in islander knowledge.   Newcomers foretold
in vision, in gossip   gouge away the vestiges
of the familiar, desecrate   the work, the fragments
of a life well-lived   for the sake of others
for joys, wars. Stood   in place, Shattered Dreams.
Industrial sheet metal,   deep black pool lights,
sensual lingerie-clad   mannequins stood on
front stoop, many lewd   sentries over north bay
road, bawdy silhouettes   declaring a new order
for the islanders, one   seeing nothing of them
reflected. Newcomers   remove baloney sandwiches,
cheap beer, replace   them with badly done
haggis, tatties, neeps.   Guido is certain these
are moves made of   warring parties, motives
brought from outside,   waged on a past
perhaps not long dead,   but not living here.
Weeks empty out into   timeless drift, envelops
multiplicity of islanders   in metastasizing change.

Pelee Islander Two   sachets proudly around
to the gentle water   nearest gull rocks, slips
into port with gentle   thud, guest meets land.
Ivan rests on bench   with Carrianne, beholds
another landing, hopes   this arrival holds him,
ila to make war   with the malefactors.
Mechanical chatter   cut by gull cries,
repetition of water   on shoreline rocks,
the parade of cars   commences, arrivals pour
from the ferry's belly.   Above buzz of itinerate
cars, people from shore   to shore bagpipes course
from pickup speakers,   Rowdy Roddy Piper descends
the ferry ramp, early   match card entrance
with namesake music,   these Green Hills
of Tyrol proclaims   their ila has arrived.
Shuffling people   pay little heed to
Piper's raucous entrance,   spare an empty nod,

a side smile at   his slow roll in
his truck, windows   down, wheeling past ferry
company office, Ivan   connects gaze with Piper
recognizes his living   legend before him, grand
Saint of Piper's Pit,   vanquisher of the Snuka,
tamer of Adonis' mane,   master of the Sleeper,
Piper was known to   all the people's church
adherents, Sunday service   regular, body and spirit,
and now living truck   driving saviour landed here,
entering as if one   grand seasonal entrance.
They watch as he   slow rolls his way
to the Westview Tavern,   the new gathering point
across from the dock,   awaiting awènik arrivals and
on rare occasion lamenting   some regret-filled departures.
Carrianne stands first, insists   Ivan follow her, he
is hesitant, concerns over   heroes, real life failures
of dreams one holds   for living, breath drawing
figures of romantic wars.   She repeats Irma's vision,
says Creation has made   the path they walk,
true gifts are those   that are prayed for,
to fear them is   the forced rejection of
blessings, an acceptance   of a curse, betrothal
to the darkness as   it finds a new dwelling.
This Ivan agrees with.   After time to let
their arriving ila settle   into a stream of island
time, they cross to   cheerless crusted white
wood tavern long on   watch over the man-
made Neutral Sea port.   Inside, Chilliwack
croons *there's no time   for changing plans, I
must believe it's in   your hands.* Boastful guitar,
keyboards lands question   like quartz, full-bodied
lustrous, but hidden from   daylight, and then blasted
in through ceiling-mounted   speakers. Ivans struts through
the front doors as if   entering ringside, nearly dances,
replays Piper's struts between   crowd throngs, beneath lights
of all the ancestors   descending all at once.

Piper sits bar side,   holds steady an audience
confesses a long travel   for a condensed visit
to the island. Tourists   and ferry workers talk

but not recognize him,   they react affectionately
to the handsome man,   well-built and talkative
he is the visitor   that brochures are hewn
to attract. He does   not acknowledge Ivan
nor Carrianne's entrance,   he conveys showmanship
in exaggerated gestures,   exemplifying his nature,
face over chitaninu, bold   charisma over brute strength.
Piper, seated among others,   embraces people over places,
pulls outsiders onto his   path for shared moments.

Ivan nestles onto stool   near Piper, needles his
attention with head nod,   orders club soda, knock
knuckles against wood top.   Carrianne stands off, aloof
and watching as Ivan   wanders between hero worship
and rescuing their island.   Perhaps drink, perhaps rough
thud against bar top,   draws Piper's attention.
He lets a fourth mate   from the ferry finish
their story about fighting   freighter crews in Sandusky,
the ceremony pugnacious,   overworked awènik pilot
their lives towards, crash   against, and create cruel
hierarchies that guide them   through their restless glide
between land and people.   Piper is at ease
with them, moves honest   like between beer mug
and laughter. Ivan holds   small disappointment,
finds Piper as outsider   that he is, feels
the stories shared here   at the stop-over bar
for boat crews, tourists   are about basic survival
in a world every islander   rejected, the outside, mainland,
the unrelenting lights   beyond. His hero undone
into transient ila, one   unrooted from land, one
strange as the golden   ones Irma's visions saw.
Foreboding knowledge   dawns in Ivan
that on rare occasion   the gods we praise
will land among us,   and their distant wars
become ours. Irma's vision,   like all visions before
are warnings, alms tendered   from a tattered creation.
Ivan shoulders that weight   of living working class
gospels come to life,   and how they gather
in the distance through   crackle white fuzz dimensions
of far-off television signals,   and coalesce in shadows

when eyes are focused   on the show's spectacle
and day-dreams fail   at dictating the fraught
with the change, outside   world can often bring.

Fourth mate ends story   with baptism of sorts,
the Neutral Sea washing   away conflict, cold waters
pulling dark medicines from   ilaok, their cardless match
completed by a bump   every witness could feel
coming, the story important   to the grand sell
of all of it.   The life, almighty essence
of how battles and   fixes are shared histories
even when the details   differ in specific ways.
"And you?" Piper asks   Ivan who yammers out
word islander and notes   his ancestors knew
war alongside Prince,   hunted in the wetlands
before the pumphouses   parched them into fields.
Piper spouted that Ivan's   lineage is more sturdy
than the island beneath   them all, bellered out
a chest-deep laugh that   drew in those gathered.
A bottle swig led   to complements sung to
the beauty of Pelee,   to forests he beheld
from the ferry deck,   cool spice of lake
water, and the cormorants   cutting the waters' surface,
a gull cry of day   dream in Great Lake
beyond. Piper toasts to   pumphouses, ferries, and Ivan.
Adds that he is here   hunting for a lost friend.

Another numbered ferry mate   starts in, naming Detroit
his fight card location.   The pronouncement calling
for another round, Piper   indicates he is responsible
for paying with twirl   of his finger. Tilts back
on his stool, prodding   on the storyteller. He
settles back as, jeers   at mention of a Shiek
arises, an improbable   accumulation of events
and equally impossible   endings. Ivan listens like
he does to the priests,   politeness, quiet, and patience.

Commotion of some new   entrants, Carrianne falls in
from the background,   Guido and Ambrose burst in
and history stops for   the unfolding hysteria of

the present. Guido flustered   by rage, proclaims loudly
the golden usurpers have   setup at the winery.
He hollers his rage   and struts to curtain
around horseshoe of   bar stools, whole house
attention falls on him,   fail Piper, whose gaze
rests forward. Hesitation   fills the bar room.
"Gold, you say?" Piper   asks, slow like. He
retrieves his sunglasses   from his shirt rim,
puts them on before   turning to face Guido.
He confirms the lustre   of gold. "Lusty?" queries
Piper and he rubs   provocative hands across
his own chest. Guido   nods. Piper tilts chin
towards the arrivals,   asks about a woman.
Guido affirms this then   adds about her cigar.
Piper removes sunglasses,   reveals eyes ablaze in
frenetic energy, Ivan sees   the moments before first
bump, the tinderstick to   ignite both pop, battle.
He rises from the bar   boldly demands where winery
is to elation of ferry   crew, fawning over drinks.
Piper states this vacation   is work of sorts,
the blowoff, the final   battle of an arc
made of dark matches   stretched out two nations
wide. This winery shall   be the show finale,
the match to set   the world sufficiently right.

Piper leads the bar   patrons out into light
of early evening. He   encourages Guido, Ambrose
along with emphatic sweeps   of his hands, whole
body urgency for them   to lead the way.
Ivan is half disappointed   half relieved destiny pulled
them from the bar   and into brewing tempest
that swirls around them,   heralded in vision, stoked
by ceremony. Ivan   a vessel for action,
with a few nods   and even fewer words.
Sunlight, revving engines   slamming of car doors,
Piper's white stallion of   truck growls into line
behind the winery work   van and they burn
off, white chalk gravel   punched into air, grind
of pressure and weight   into limited earth, way
follows the shore straight   to the south, ferry

like a skyline punctuated   with painted cormorant
outlines. Gravel lots and   a grand abandoned hotel
sputter by the caravan.   Cormorants perched on rocks
lurking a dozen feet   out in the lake,
crane head and wings   witness a cacophonous
parade of awènik enroute   to an evitable showdown
They flowed into winery   parking lot, wailing
of pipes, and drone   of pure Detroit muscle,
as his half-ton Ford   halts with a harsh
crunch of rock under   foot. Creaking of doors
as Piper and entourage   emerge from slow-roll,
cut-off of entrance music   follows closing slams of
car doors. Piper stands   tall, puts on sunglasses.
In distance, over winery   building, he delays
and then professes that   what he pursues rests,
waits for him opposite   of the wine pavilion.
Through the half-full   parking lot, Piper heads
the march, kilt red   like chkënakw, his wings
let loose and black   leather jacket his shield,
he struts past vines   pruned for their harvest.

Through cavernous pavilion,   emptied of awènik, workers
vacated bar and toppled   vintage island-themed artifacts,
Piper pauses near barstools,   picks up golden glitter
and silken strands of   ahtuhwixèkën smothering
the surfaces. Finger tip   coated, he fixes upon
traces of his quarry.   Coaxes the others should
follow, and the poor   into the vast veranda,
the ears filled with   grinding rhythms of synth
pop love making for   money kind of music.
They all stand behind   Piper. Guido is first
to his side, witnesses   workers lined up on
the dozen barbeques   his customers rent by
half hour, and smell   and smoke of meat
being grilled en masse.   In middle of them
all parading about   in gold and black
jumpsuit, Nkuli Punkw   notes newcomers arrival.
He swaggers about to   music, seizes hold of
a package of meat,   in muscular push, hands
it off to a worker.   Nkuli Punkw waits quietly.

Piper launches into sprint   slingshots himself onto
patio below, few gathered   flee for safer ground,
highland ila tosses leather   jacket aside, languidly strides
forward. Each step he   preens in the lake
crosswind. Guido ask   Ivan if this grips
him like Fort Wayne's   No Holds Barred card
a few years back.   Ivan nods because he
knows that true gospels   tend to replay themselves,
mirror life and fiction,   final matches on any
card are darker and   less designed than you
would ever hope or   wish to believe in.

Close to barbeque pit,   twenty-four carat woman
cuts off Piper. In   crisp evening light, Ivan
believes her elegant,   strength near danger, in
stilt-like muscular form   she holds against her dress.
With smoke bellowing forth,   the woman was nature
poisoned, turned to threat,   looming elegant sensual threat,
a form leaving Ivan   with surging lusty pangs.
She demands to know   who sent him. Through
her billows of smoke,   Piper says he hunts
alone and acts at   his own personal accord.
Marlena places her hand   against his chest. Hot
Rod held back, he   sidesteps her glare, builds
distance, boldly shows his   disdain for her presence.
"I ain't looking for   you, Lady," he launches
with a highland bull   glare. He brushes off
his shoulder announces   ahtuhwixèkën is worse
than glitter because it   smells like glands most
women don't have. He   demands she releases Dustin,
and a lint roller,   all their weird dander
has made a mess   of his tartan and shirt.
Piper marches towards pit,   she motions to catch
him as he walks   away, his back turned.
Nkuli Punkw rasps out   a lust-riddled need
to have the kilted   man come to him.
Marlena stalks after Piper,   ahtuwok silent, waits, watches.

Piper runs hand through   blonde mane of hair,
preens before striking out   at the spirit jobber

that holds his friend.   Whole smile, a warning,
begins highland ila question   "Where ya been, Dustin?"
Production of shatter dreams,   steps to Piper, package
of bratwursts clenched in   cupped hands, three-quarters
anxiety as he inhales   loud enough for Ivan
to hear, demands Piper   say his real name
"Nkuli Punkw," he hisses,   pushes bratwursts into
Piper's face. "Say it,   and you can stay
for our sausage party."   Piper slaps bratwursts from
Golden Ila's outstretched   hand, wags his index
finger before him. Nkuli   Punkw strikes first,
a crossbody chop that   chases pheasants from nearby
brush. Guido sees winery   workers scatter to edges
of the pit. There   they perch and watch
as these ilaok exchange   growing frenetic impacts, each
one bone deep, each   one near to shaking
the earth beneath them.   Two brawlers unleashed,
berating flesh with violent   flesh, neither one giving
ground. Piper straight punch,   countered with a sunset
power bomb. Eye gouges,   recoveries, spine busters hit.
barbeques over turned,   thunderous chair smashes,
choke holds broken, sleepers   breeched, recovered from.
Piper breaks the swinging   neckbreaker, survives Final
Cut from Golden One.   Piper grapples with Sleeper,
believes he is going   over, the battle ending.
He wheels through struggle,   surfaces facing Marlena, who
has approached the battle   hushedly. Piper holds Nkuli
Punkw tightly, senses his   foe falling to sleep.
The Golden One's arms   grow near limp, legs
barely holding ground, quiet   anticipation from gallery
the end being near.   Marlena billows forth cloud
of smoke, an unhuman   cry that shatters windows
of the pavilion, shocked   Piper loosens sleeper hold
slightly and his foe   draws strength in moment.
Smoke lingers around Piper,   he feels Nkuli Punkw
stir sharply, struggles to   hold this slipping edge
of triumph He fails.   Nkuli Punkw fumbles away,
both ilaok heave in   breath, sweat and blood
drenched the quiet   lingers above. Golden One,
he launches handful of   ahtuhwixèkën, luminous

dust. Piper sells a   hard fall felt from
afar, releases the Golden   One. He rises like
a surging, unsteady xkuk.   He strikes Piper with
a brutal sunset flip   powerbomb. Leaves Roddy
loose limbed on ground.   Marlena exchanges glare
with the Golden One.   Nodding, he wobbles to
straight stand, grabs limp   weight of Piper, lifts
and hauls him to   a huddle of gas grills.

Nkuli Punkw hoists   a Piper loosed limbed
to unsteady feet, held   upright between two
barbeques. Piper's mind   rolls bathed in arena
light memories, battles   fought far too long
ago. Ivan, Kelly, them   all witness evisceration
without commentary,   Sunday mornings come
to flesh before them,   dull body thuds, fore-
arm chops. Their hope   hamstrung before them,
He stumbles back to   the copper still centre
of the plaza, bloodied   black and gold hand
rings the hollow vessel   before he rises, runs
at the splayed Piper   delivering soul-splicing blow
to his foe's loins,   his finisher landed. Ivan
reminds Guido of seeing   the Shatter Dreams clear
from a Terre Haute card.   Ambrose has been haunted
since, grimaces as Piper   deflates to hard ground.
Exhaustion over takes   the Golden One, he
coughs, slumps to ground.   Grind of a winless victory,
temporary as pain is,   three deep breaths. Rest.
He lunges for nearby   bratwurst package, tosses
them atop Piper's limp   body, hisses he'll need
them now. Watchers gasp   when Piper offers silence.
A blown kiss from   the victor, battle ended.
Marlena strides up to   Nkuli Punkw, scoops him
to his feet, supports   his exit. Synth pop
continues belting out into   the darkening night sky
The dark spirits retreat   to night in forest.

Ambrose and Kelly are   first to Piper's aid.
Guido hollers after his   employees, hostile scoldings
for opportunistic turnings,   opines the ferry leaves

tomorrow and he hopes   the traitors reserve seats.
Ferry workers descend upon   the debris, look to
the pieces of a fellow   ilaok's precisely human loss.
Carrianne retrieves jacket,   glasses. Ivan receives them.
The women lift Piper   to his feet, drag
him semi-conscious   from the pit shambles.
Carrianne asks softly about   Piper's sole plan being
to simply pummel   dark spirits from his
friend. Between wheezes   exhaustion, whirling pain
he chuckles. Mumbles   clear as he can
fate and dumb luck   have forged his life
thus far, big plans   were things he borrowed.

Ivan lingers as they   drag off their ila,
leather jacket on shoulders,   but not slipped on,
sunglasses in hand he   hadn't believed in loss.
Recalls Piper's surety,   then the sunglasses
how and when he   wore then. He wondered.
Nervous, Ivan puts on   the glasses. Nekanemën.

Canto Naxa

Pètapàn rolled up   to rose gold lake.
Piper, stirs bleary eyed.   He balances groggy sleep
and waking, his head   buzzing, neck wrenched,
dull pain that hangs   on, presses one into
retreat from its dull   heaviness. Lake gentle,
soft-edged waves   unfurl sly into ripples.
A calming hand on   naked rim of his back,
he awakens, fight   lingers in faint thrum
of pain. Carrianne   plies the space above
him, clears dark   medicines still clung
to him. She explains   nothing, he seeks
none. Rises, looks   to the lake. They are
in the shed behind   the shell of the old
Casino at island's   edge. Electric carnival
of the distant shore   shrunk to pencil
sketches of how   rollercoasters slide
along paths of light.   Awake, the day hurts.

Following him, Carrianne   confirms he slept late.
The island folk speak   of despair, fear after
Piper's last fall and   public make-out session
of the victors. Spirit   of dark spaces, of
lustrous metals, hunger   for what can't be
owned, no matter   the desire, no matter
belief, the earth   belongs to no one,
even in parts. Such   beliefs spiral to violence.
Kwèn'shùkwënay   defend us. Daunting amount
of time has passed   since they heaved water,
blisters that dare not   break the surface. Waters
quiet, skeletal like the   slumbering amusement
park. Brackish she   calls the air, stagnant
Piper thinks. They   walk, prodding small
hope with small talk   into new day sun.

Ivan, rests beneath   xaxakw beside road,
mesh-woven lawn   chair, its lowland tartan
pattern pierces pastoral   green like wisawtayas
perched on a branch.   Piper says the beating

was less painful than   match night in Philly,
which explains the ache   and also the endurance,
knowing that there can   never be not enough
of how one struggles   through, simply does.
Ivan produces sunglasses   Piper dropped last night.
Through them they have   both witnessed the truth
of Nkuli Punkw's being,   seen neon pulses of
dark medicine through   him and her, driving
their true selves towards   cruelest actions, terrors
in human form. Raw   hungry lust forever
groping at the world.   Through these sunglasses
visible are twisted   faces of pulsating
light, shadow, mostly   shadow, storms spun
from flesh. Hers is   hidden behind an L.A.
feminine beauty, cliché.   He decorates copies
the shadows, copies   the swirls of golden
light. Two different   faces, same demon.
This dark medicine lashes   from their bodies, yet
does not leave. Through   glasses, they crackle.

Ivan admits he saw   the possessed duo after
Piper had laid still   after Shattered Dreams
ended their fight.   Piper's shades found
beneath picnic tables,   Ivan beheld their dark
possession as the two   departed, backs turned
to battlefield, defeated   powerless and battered.
From there, survivors   secured, they fled
to safety of southern   sacred ground, rested.
Dark glasses returned,   he recons them
potential relief   for his relentless
head-busting pain   amplified beneath
with each surge   of saccharine daylight.
Ivan points out   past Pelee's edge
to beyond Middle   Island, a broad rather
than pointed gesture.   Piper puts them on.

Along the horizon south   of them, he sees
the darkening ridges   of restless medicine,
hungry medicine, dark   medicine, he knows
it well enough. Shows,   workman's eyes, tired

but resolved at what   shall pass, work need
be done, and Piper   the only one prepared
and capable, solitary   fighter in a singular war.
He repeats aloud, he   knows it well enough

Piskewëni comes on   faster, congealing
miasma along horizon,   they muster in the galley
of Guido's stilted RV.   Piper silent, Ivan guides
the others on events   unseen, golden oldies
from clock radio   candy coats his words:
sweet, sweet city woman,   I can see your face,
I can hear your voice,   I can almost touch
you. They take all   hard facts, faint radio
in quiet audience.   Eager, they turn attention
from Ivan to him,   inviting warrior to speak,
Piper from atop counter   crosses from silence
to speech with a smirk   like sasapëlehële before
impact. He has said   less than he knows.
he is leading without   ancestors' guides. Walking
without speaking words   honestly of your path,
is base. He speaks   calling ancestors back.

Begins with Stanley   Toombs, a somewhat
father, cruel as a rail   cop could be, enough
for son to leave home,   live in high prairie
hostels, scrape money   from odd jobs, make
a forgotten era, when   Piper flows from Roderick,
becomes the bagpipe   playing maniac, battler
of fierce powerful men   from nation to nation.
from arenas to barrooms,   from antennas feeding
tv sets, their Sunday   services of good versus
evil. As he spoke   Ivan became certain
Piper's words were   a new gospel, a testament
worth believing, tales   of how one brawls
against a hungry world,   of how wanting leads
to contests that often   breaks one in soul
deep ways. Leaves with   lives changed, paths lost.

Feuds are common   as friendship, change
is the perpetual way   a wrestling life plays

out. Nkuli Punkw   was once Dustin,
fast friend, blood brother,   all before Winnipeg.

On a northern circuit   money-maker tour,
a small house match   versus Saskamoose Mangler,
he missed a high rope   maneuver, mis-landed
atomic cross-body drop   into a row of aunties
from near north end.   He should have known
continuing was wrong,   but the money counted
far more than anything   should. So, he finished
Saskamoose before a crowd   silenced by a violent
misfire. And the aunties   moaned in crushed
bone agony, looked on   as Dustin posed above
a prone Saskamoose.   He played his role,
the pay was healthy,   delivered hurriedly
for every witness there   felt abysmal evil stir.

Ahtuhxkwe caught   up to Dustin after
hours, a tavern in   her territories,
the near north side,   great nesting den
of bold medicines,   mèthìk or welhìk
in the city. Alone,   he acceded to her
advances. Later Piper   learned, his arrival
and bartender chat,   carousing with patrons,
they spoke of Dustin's   departure with her,
back booth a familiar   den for her fawning
last seen lost men,   guilty, they held sure
of darkest mèthìk.   Their delinquencies
unknown, her actions   unseen, a dutiful mercy.
A vigilante, timeless,   spirit world vestige
has never left us,   lingered on as watchers
as people grew in time,   in population, in ego.
The old ways dimmed   in their waxing fires,
obfuscating good and   evil in overwhelming
propagation of hungers.   Hidden not put out,
they smolder, and one   spark, one tongue
leapt from a dark city   night, consumed Dustin.
Piper could not find   him, nor would patrons
talk about where she   came from, where she
could have gone. He   is shown the corner

they were seen in.   In dim light, he
finds empty bottles,   sand-fine golden
dust, celestial blonde   ahtuhwixèkën, a scent
of rich smoke,   sweet forest musk.
No one dare utter   her name. He departs.

Two weeks post   Winnipeg, Piper works
a Sacramento Sunday   afternoon show, last
minute change puts   Saskamoose upon
his card. They battle   in a middle bout,
neither spotlight, nor   sleeper, it is work.
They battle, trudging   through choregraphed
chops, suplexes, rakes,   thundering clotheslines.
Piper lingers on Dustin,   his lasting absence,
the match a blur,   a measured dance between
pain and work, each   act for selling it,
Piper locked on cost   Dustin must have paid
to do that small   house show money maker.
After the match, they   meet up in backlot
of the arena. Piper   offers American Spirits
to Mangler, a gift   mixed with request.
Two ilaok at rest,   testing each other's
mythologies, sharing   their ritual smokes,
Saskamoose chats   of his northern city
first, the rarity of   recent small shows,
kindness of pro   outsiders to pull
in crowds from south   side neighbourhoods.
He mentions Dustin's   match and mishap,
a twisting diving   cross body he drove
into those aunties   in attendance. Then
he fought on like   it was all show,
their injuries a side   hustle, quietly ignored,
while he moved to   big money moments.
Callousness labelled   business, a colonizer
spirit, insidious from   its root, intolerable
in spaces welcoming   to Saskamoose.

Ahtuhxkwe came   to him. Agile and
silent like all her   sisters, elegant
as stars drifting   past treetops, seeing

70

all below, judging   preparing her justice.
Ahtuhxkwe came   to him in anger
vengeful anger, yet   Saskamoose viewed
Dustin alive in L.A.,   three long days before.
Dustin transformed,   dominated by dark
medicine, had become   a mongrel of gold
dust and dark lust,   with him a lady
belching fires of dying   rage for betrayed,
murdered women and   children she hunted
since kishux first shone   upon the turtle shell
world. Long ago she   came for a twisted
man, wielder of bad   medicines and he
seduced her. Left her   with lasting energies
of lust and rage, for   by her nature she
had to kill him.   Yet she could not.
Many ilaok have fallen   into earth from her
touch. Each necessary   act leaving scars,
ones torn open in   her hunting of Dustin.
She calls him Nkuli   Punkw for traces
of gold flakes that   flow in his shadow
poisoning, sparkles   like a spurious night
sky. All things he   touches, he lusts over,
Dustin has become   a vessel for darkness,
bleak, gold-punctuated   pitay, a consuming foam.
Ahtuhxkwe broken   becomes beautiful Marlena,
she clutches at tobacco   to cure the illness.
Cigar smoke trails   follow her timeless promise
turned curse. Mangler   heard of Calgary terror,
city men and women,   molested, these colonial crimes
descended from toxic   coupling of two improbable
personae, manufacture   one loathsome monster.

Old ones knew this   would occur, sensed
a change in spirit,   slow like ice shelves
gliding over rock,   grinding earth until
a change so deep   that creation becomes
unrecognizable. These   two united dark spirits
would enjoin, twist   medicines together,
rise as treaties were   ignored, righteous path
lost. To their great   grandchildren, terror

would come hungry   to consume their world.
These old ones left   his relations a means
to see the medicine   of Ahtuhxkwe
from his uncle who   walked in the way
of Memphis King,   Saskamoose managed
the sunglasses Piper   holds before islanders
gathered in the RV   kitchen, gloom growing.
Saskamoose returned   north, stated this next
fight was not his.   Fine cards are made
by visions, good sense.   He was of neither.

Guido asks about others   lost to growing evil.
Piper falls into a sing   song, the freefall wide
and made of places,   cities, mundane, exotic.
Piper faced Nkuli   Punkw in Fargo, fled
to Omaha after him,   picked over Terre Haute
found little but injury,   loss and lingering shadow.
That same path brought   Piper here, to battle
them for one final   time, to return balance
to an ancient spirit,   to release a sinner,
friend hard awash in   an unproportional hell,
and vanquish a spreading   evil, free them all.

Irma calls out ahtu   visions, kick mark pain,
dull in the chest.   Crisp streamers of neon
light wrapped shadow   and Hamm's sullen tavern
at the centre. Beacon,   the gyre's bleak heart,
there evil found its   fountain mouth. There
the place to close   off the evil. Clear
apparitions of kilted   man and an assault
to end this invasion,   liberate their island,
change this darkest   path, restore calm.
Piper shakes his head,   states spiritual sights
are fine but don't   win fights, they all
had watched his butt   kicked the day before.
Tension drops silence   over the trailer,
conversation and   confessions brought
to heel then linger,   Lightfoot on the radio
sometimes I think it's   a sin when I feel
like I'm winning   but I'm losing again.

Kelly's voice breaks in   before Sundown repeats
agrees with Piper by   nod, punctuates that
with near question   about Nkuli Punkw,
how it is not   him Piper finds fight
with, it is dark   medicines beyond him,
a shadow illness not   soul deep, instead one
that can be chased   from part of creation.
Piper drops coy smile,   emphatically slaps
counter behind him.   Liberated from brooding
dread, he surges with   defiant hope, shakes
trailer with potential   energy. Piper pleads
for more from Kelly.   Moves attention on
her. She holds up   a glass bottle hued
bold Webstad orange   mpisun, as if wsike
born into awènik hands,   nurtured, honed under
glass into healing   mpisun, Pelee distilled
and brought to lips,   elixir of life clung
to the same land   battered by Neutral Sea
tempests, pierced   tortured by winter winds.
Kelly tells Piper that   this buckthorn healed
him, it is survival,   strength of creation.

Piper collects bottle   holds it against light
sees in its chalky   pulp glow, churning
motions, eddies like   living mpi, at ease
but not at rest,   light resonating
from within. Between   fingers it buzzed
with life. He smiled   like when first arrived,
Carrianne nods to Ivan,   whose return confirms
that Irma's visions still   run true, and hope
sprouts rich from the   ground beneath them.

Canto Newa

Piskapamùkòt returns   and punches shores
distant to life, rich   lights awoken from
midday rest, opacity   brought on oversoon
in thickening storms.   In tempests, lights
shine brightest. Sky   above all, first six
heavens aflame in   what power awènik
could cast from below.   Upwards, constantly
upwards, searching   for saviours, for god,
for answers that come   by no clear measure,
that a sky can be   anything much beyond
an unclear medium,   an incomplete metaphor,
always unattainable.   The sky undulates
with the light of many   reaching up, longing
for an improbable   immaculate response.
And in the darkness   Ivan, Guido, Kelly,
and Carrianne   sat with their answer,
Piper bandaged up,   bathed in waters
of churned up waves   from chafed Neutral Sea.
Tempest breaks in above,   tracked in by Nkuli
Punkw, his cursed state   a lure, this island
its inevitable aerie.   In certainty Hamm's old
bar was the locus of   the gathering dark medicine.
Ivan and the assemblage   break camp in amplifying
tempest, Piper alone in   his truck, sea buckthorn
vials in leather jacket   pockets, glasses latched
on shirt collar, his   sight lingers on lake.
The carnival of lights   has burned to life
in the distance, night   descended early, skies build.
And with a crash   of light, and wind,
far off thunder blast   those lights vanished
into encroaching   shadows. Darkness
consumed the edges,   match time had come.
Piper pops chewing gum,   pushes convoy to motion.
Past light the convoy   of vehicles pushes north
to the magnetic centre   to which the mustering
darkness gathers, crawls   up Centre Dyke road
past reaching branches of   nushèmakòk, ran hard
beneath their shadows,   and the rustling shifts

of chëmàmsàk past   settling gravel and powder
stirred up in their   transit. Ivan pictures
them in action scene   romance, Piper's stance
into the wind gust   near-night of movie
final, blonde hair mop   majestic in its motion,
night sheer cormorants   cutting waves and gales
riding above lake top,   razor through this darkness.
Island at sleep around   them, past stillwater canals,
and the unlighted airport,   unattended fire station,
gravel road ping-pongs   and they know peace
neither marks their passage   nor prepares for them
to arrive. Three white   cars cut this night.

Past the northside   pumphouse, clear of
the old town marina,   and the three meek
store fronts alongside   Scudder's only paved road,
they surge to collective   stop. Headlights reveal
pishkok moving through   nearby tree tops, preparing
for their nightfall feast.   Over car engine chirps
they can make out   the same music from
the winery. In volume   it waged war with
the retreating day. Ivan   sees them first, resting
up Hamm's old place,   black pool lights, spin
of them against sheet   metal and Shattered Dreams
backlit in neon blues,   greens. Colours noticed
through Piper's sunglasses   A phalanx of mannequins
caught in pulses of   light, rotations of disco
ball flare patterns, stood   silent in front windows.
Upon the covered stoop   a deep-cut darkness.
There they rest upon   Muskoka chairs, reign
over the nearby parking   lot, pulsating trill
of electronic music, bird   song without soul,
blasted through speakers,   maybe a stereo, hidden
in that darkness. Marlena   demonstrates ambivalence,
idle release of smoke,   relaxed metronome twitch
of leg crossed over   leg. Nkuli Punkw stands
as the first of them,   Ambrose leaves his car.
For a moment, their   music runs into silence
and sounds of pishkok   feeding surrounds them all.

Their righteous ila steps   into the night, slides
his sunglasses on,   tilts his stern glance
to the dark usurpers   upon their stolen perch.
He retrieves bagpipes   from behind his seat,
and in stride positions   them with shoulder shrug.
In passing gusts Piper   walks forward, pipes held
under arm against wind,   rage, the chants, pops
of electric machine rhythm.   Atmosphere ricochets
between imported and   natural melodies, stutters.
He wields the wails   from within the bag,
walks forward across road   forcing Green Hills of
Tyrol from the pipes,   each breath, drone, push
a meditation, a clear   headed memory of what
went wrong the night   before, what could not
turn wrong tonight.   He pushes his song
louder and the island   rushes away, leaving him
with his breath song   and the wind beseeching
him to march forward.   Step, push, breathe, focus.
Nkuli Punkw leaves his   post, nudges toward Piper
in shoulder tense steps.   Piper stops near lawn.
He lays the pipes   down to his left,
takes three steps forward   then spits out gum.
Piper hollers at them,   defiant as a healed man
come to face his   foe and target again.
"I have come here   to kick ass and chew
bubble gum and I'm   all out of bubble gum."

Piper charges forward,   cannonading muscle sprint,
speed earned by digging   into soil, exploding through
gravity and air. Ivan   has appreciated the like
from tv set distance,   and is taken by
the raw power as   Piper surges across road.
Nkuli Punkw flexes chest   through tight golden shirt,
steps down and forward   to face Piper, accept
another of the battles   permeating between ilaok.
They are màxkok, quiet   in speech, quaking ground
as they walk, preened,   previous wars commence as
though ends are myth,   the present enduring long
past a welcome moment.   Their fight, this battle
so natural to the world,   that no end comes.

Ivan swears he feels   the indurate bodies meet,
a deep soul level thud   that shakes creation beyond
mere physical proportions,   manëtuwàk shifted in
sky and on earth,   shoved from their repose
they witness as ilaok   clash, unfettered from tv
wave containment this   carnage unfolding through
degrees to shape sky   and earth. No spot
to follow, these men   grapple as if might
itself was in short   supply. Ivan, Ambrose,
and fellow spectators   stood by their cars,
their engines left running,   lights engulfed the field
of battle. Nkuli Punkw   blazed with unnatural light.
And in their struggle   Piper holds them, seizes
land from Nkuli Punkw.   Marlena breathes languid
smoke, even against wind   holds steady nebulous, aloft.
Ambrose suggests to Ivan   she idles like deer
along the tree line.   Preparing tentative steps
in flight, in frenzy,   elegant in her focus.

Piper launches his rival   lurching backwards with
a head smash, followed   by open handed chop.
He leers at the dark   one, lifts sun glasses
from his face, drops   them aside. Deep cutting
glare of an alais   before the goring attack.
Piper struts to meet   Nkuli Punkw, delivers
forearm chops, jabs,   a frenzy to push back
his prey, take hold   of lost ground, punch
through exhaustion, pain.   Frenzy from endurance
the Dark One stumbles   back, Piper slings
his leather jacket aside,   then lands boot kick
to his target's chest.   Nkuli Punkw crashes into
porch support, crack then   dull body crash across
the porch. He stands up   to meet Piper, sluggish
and limp, throws loose   punch, trapped in hand
by Piper and wielded   to cast an Irish whip
slingshot of Nkuli   Punkw into porch chairs.
Marlena unfurls a surge   of thick smoke, back
lit by car lights,   covered in choking musk,
our ila wavers in   the miasma, wheezes, stalls.

"You should have kept   the shades," Dark One
says, "the colour suits   you." With choke hold
he raises him above   ground. Sigh. Hungry glare.
Nkuli Punkw launches   Piper into sound system
and the horrid grind   of electric bop gore
peaks then dies out.   Leaves the atmosphere
with car engines and   winds gusts that clobber
upper tree branches,   pepper the bleak sky
beyond. Piper is stunned,   breathes in urgent heaves,
lays flat against turned   over chairs, loose detritus
of the match. Dark One   leans into Marlena's
open mouth smoke-infused   kiss. Surges with power.
Carrianne senses thickened   shadows behind her, night
becoming still. A quickening   of the smothering darkness.
Piper brought to his   feet by Nkuli Punkw,
moves like a xkuk,   runs lustful hands across
his own chest, ends   in a mocking flourish.
He sets Piper up   like a mannequin, slack,
balanced against gravity and   against time, steps back.
Nkuli Punkw gloats, lingers   then launches into attack.
Piper limps backwards   wakens enough to behold
the Dark One's convergence.   Piper catches him square
in mid stride, catapults   Nkuli Punkw onto shoulders
into an airplane spin   that shoots Nkuli Punkw
into the replica crowd   behind him, white plastic
parts shattering around him,   the wall stops him.
And both ilaok search   for footing, Piper heaving
for breath is first   upright. He fixates upon
Marlena, indignant and edging   away from the exchange,
he broadcasts a burning   sun smile, beaming that
this moment isn't hers,   cocksure that his heroics
will take this time   around. He turns, discovers
the Dark One off   balance, dumb from the spin
Piper raises Nkuli Punkw   with a knee lift kick,
and backs off, admiring   approaching ends. Pauses.

Piper unleashes a flurry   of frenzied fists, chops
and Nkuli Punkw stumbles   numb and punching air
confused attack, recoiling   against shadow, fighting ends
that shall not be   averted. Piper scoops sea

buckthorn bottle from　his pocket, belts a pull
of mpisun then plants　a mouth kiss upon
dazzled Nkuli Punkw, spits　sea buckthorn into
his mouth. The Dark One　swats madly and misses.
Piper subdues him　slaps a suplex on him
and hammers Nkuli Punkw　into hard ground. Piper
tears the golden speckled　jumpsuit from Dustin,
leaving him bare to　world. He hurls bunched
up remains at Marlena.　Before he manages to
catch her, she bellows　a bray of desperate terror,
bounds off into shadows.　Piper certain the island
will contain her, what　remains of contaminated
dark medicines, he will　end the discord soon.

He bends down to　Dustin, feels dead weight
against the dried lawn　of long departed Hamm's
lasting island presence. He　feels for pulse, stands
up satisfied and launches　the prairie smile through
exhausted return to posture.　Heavens extended above,
reveal growing numbers　of alànkòk. Receding dark
medicine, with each ignition　of distant spirit, ebbs into
the essence of Pelee　before outside punctured
their world, brough distant　wars before them all.
Behind her Carrianne senses　calm, turns to witness
an open field in dusk　light. Dim outlines float
against the night, perhaps　chikënëmuk, likely pheasants.
blaring car headlights　blanche the wind stirred
and debris-cluttered ground,　the island itself glows
and tick, stutter, chirr　of engines carries night,
draws the match chaos　into mechanized calm.

Kelly rushes to Dustin,　cantillates restorative song,
employs the medicines of　voice and touch, ends
to the long infernal　path that led them
all to this point.　Piper asks about Dustin's
return and recovery of　Kelly. Irma replies in
approach that they all　perceive the atmosphere
above them rejuvenated,　Dustin too shall rise.

Ivan wanders into circle   of car light, breaks
boundaries held by years   of Toledo tv broadcasts,
communicant becomes   practitioner, he crosses
to the altar and before   him the bleak carnage
of past weeks, he   sees that spirit world
remains distant mostly,   yet visits rarely, leaves
ephemera, myths, and   certainty òs›hakame
brings good and bad,   brought in chaotic waves.
Piper crosses light asks   assemblage about Marlena
the paths she took   in flight. Ambrose says
the way leads round   to Westview, tavern
and docks. Piper darts   through crowd to truck.
Carrianne arrests him   declares Ahtuhxkwe
is built from violence,   masculine brute force
only strengthens her evil   medicines. She must be
subdued through means   akin to the hunt.
The end comes through   healing and not violence.
His response is a nod   She returns his jacket
and him to truck   and he powers off
down the dark road   beyond. Red tail lights.

Guido and Ivan follow   Piper into the gauze,
alànkòk and òxehëmu   igniting billows
of dust and smoke left   in Marlena's retreat,
of headlights cutting   shadow, moving stages
through the pheasant run   soybean fields, patch
darkness of forest, long   dominions of poplars
above road and between   them and sky. Recessed
occasional porch lights   signs of awènik life
after dark, and the   settling dust of Piper
finishing Irma's vision,   faint red tail lights
through piskewëni   ahead, them in pursuit.
Around a shore bend   and they sight most
settled portion of island,   Piper's entrance point.

Before them the Pelee   Islander bobs in unsettled
waves stirred up by   southern winds, now on
the shift towards western   origins. She sleeps between
departures, her rest   portended by cabin lights,
empty parking lot, loading   docks. Large population

at the tavern across   the road, on terrace
the ferry crew watches   their arrival, Westview
tavern patio their bleachers   and beer bottles their
tolling bells. They holler   and beller as Piper
dashes past, then up   the driveway through
the vacant car loading   lot and onto pier
exiting still-running   truck. He lingers in
under truck low beams   and discerns between
his pinched fingertips   ahtuhwixèkën patches,
a near trail leading   up the loading ramp.
And he follows her   into thrumming jaundiced
light of ferry car   deck, in metallic cavern
the sound and light   echoed as if left
in the netherworld   between land and water,
unnatural to its core,   he searches cold steel
of the empty heart   of the ship. Hears
frantic hammering   of footsteps above,
and he tears off   ascending a nearby ladder,
Piper smells faint wafts   of cigar smoke, sweet
musk that decidedly   is misplaced among
diesel and acrid oil   of over-used mechanics.
He crisscrosses ship   gangways, corridors, and
vacated passenger areas.   Hearing the patter of
her footfalls on decking,   and fresh fall of
ahtuhwixèkën, vapour   trails of cigar vestiges,
Piper follows, climbing   leaping over furniture,
glaring through windows,   guessing at direction,
Marlena some few good   moves ahead of him.

Their exhaustive chase   converges upon the aft
observation deck,   Westview's shore, docks
below visible, burning life   beneath fresh night sky.
She stands defiantly   at furthest deck point,
near life jacket lockers   and long seat rows,
she breathes hard, chase   still coursing through
her. Cornered between   water and their battle
Piper huffs out that   Saskamoose says hi,
and maintains his   distance mirrors Marlena's
movement. She stares   back, and sneers as
memory burns back to   Manitoba, registers

before times, north side   hunting terrible men,
their sheer horrendous   numbers, haunt her deeply.
Piper sees glasses over   eyes, can feel glacier
cold darkness slip   free from her spirt,
infected manëtu shedding,   still threatening illness
to the island before   them. Piper knows it
is Saskamoose's way   to set creation right,
and Marlena's wicked   spirit must be pushed
from Ahtuhxkwe.   For the spirit she
is necessary in world   unbalanced through
lust, greed, evil wrought   from across waving seas,
tossed delicate balance   of treaty bctwccn all
asunder. Guardian, she   stands in where law
and moral often fail,   a manëtu gift for
creation. Great balancer,   strong as most grand
ahtu to walk the   homelands, Piper worked
out to strike like   xkuk, through surging
muscle, surprise being   mortal way to win.
With sea buckthorn   bottle held out, Piper
huffs aloud, "This is   for your healing and
theirs." He indicates   shore, inches closer
to her, pulls mouth   full of potion, musters
— is hammered   by kick hitting his
chest. Stunned Piper   teeters back, catches fall.
Dull pain tells him   punch back, and he
submits to his ilaok   self, swipes forward
at her again, barely   misses, although he
wipes buckthorn juice   across her cheek. Marlena
loses strength at touch.   Piper seizes her firmly
by nape with one   hand, pulls her nose
to nose with him.   He catches notice of
smoke and sweet earth   in her exhausted
breaths. He lingers much   longer than he knows
right or safe, and   she struggles free with
a burst of strength,   stands facing intoxicated
Piper. In her hand   she holds the sea
buckthorn bottle. She   holds before her,
exclaims, "This is your   mëtèxkwe's only egis?"
Tosses the bottle over   board. Piper motions
after it, but holds   distance, shakes head

in disbelief of   an outcome he didn't
conceive of. He is   conscious of failing.

With flick of her   fingertips she launches
her mostly burnt cigar   butt onto ship deck.
Marlena steps to   him, Piper surrenders
space backwards with   each push, steps hard
heavy against ship deck.   He knows her strength,
his chest still heavy   sore from the kick,
scrambles plans, thoughts   to subdue Marlena.
He recalls Carrianne's   warning, knows attacking
will strengthen her,   he seeks the way
that shall bring no   blows between them,
and then to drive   the dark medicines
he dances around to   her unsteady alert
overwatch of his   movement. His orbit
shifted by her form,   stunning, elegant, fine
her beauty ethereal   and beckoning danger,
he understands why   Dustin took her wiles
for lust rather than   rage and revenge.
Sheer red dress, she   stands silent but shifts
weight and place to   match Piper, keeps him
before him, steady with   stare locked to his.

Across the road he   hears shouts from patio
of the Westview.   Alerted, crew watches on
for a rematch that   they ruminated upon
after the winery bout.   Grand blowoff match
to put rest this card,   Piper relishes cheers,
and in his dance   the strength he draws
from them calms him,   and confidence floods.
Voices of ferry crew   evoke their battle yarns
of Neutral Sea baptisms,   how not all mpisun
grows from earth, he   gains awareness about.
Lakes, rivers, waters are   the largest medicines.
Piper struts, drops smile   like a loch surface
on a highland summer   day, her hand he
grabs hold of, as   if preparing to hoist
her towards first spring   of a dance, and delicate

like wraps his arm   around her exquisite
waist. Thoughts of pure   want flush through him
and he struggles to   keep still his mind,
maintain his angle,   alarmed again by power
of her darkened spirit   through soft touch of
flesh against flesh, she   follows his soft push.

"You've come to dance?"   she croons playful.
Piper smiles back, plays   at gentleman not prey
not hunter, not lustful   lover. He glides her
into a swing step   swoop, thrum of idle
ship beneath them, hint   of breeze and steady
splash of impatient   water below interlace
the rhythm of steps.   "Reality is our dance,"
Piper beams back at   her, stare unbroken.

In his arms, near   rail he nudges her
closer to edge, gaze   locked, challenged to
keep her at safe   distance than smother
her in hungry urge   driven embrace, he
sees the small smudge   of sea buckthorn still
upon her cheek, he   understands her dark
powers to be still   weakened. "Some dance,"
he says, "some lurk,   with you it's dance.
But sooner or later,   everybody pays the
Piper!" Her eyes flash   surprise, find worry.

Brisk, curt maneuver   Piper shoves Marlena
over rail. She holds   on rigidly to his
wrist and he slams   into rail, anchors weight
of them both suspended   above light studded waves
below. Their eyes   locked again, hers burn
with neons and swirled   angst of spirit gone
wrong, bristling rage   of will to survive.

"Between the two of   you, I believe the
good one swims." He   blows a smooch in
her face and sees   fractured pools of
rich black ahtu eyes   stare back, the neon
swirls of spirit force   bristle forward up her

arm, and what he   is certain is true
to Ahtuhxkwe's   kind soul, he discerns
a turn he has seen   few times in matches,
and blows a kiss   back that he knows
is resplendent with   thanks. She releases
his wrist as dark   energy waves surge to
his arm. She tumbles   and Piper apprehends
in her descent four   decks below, her legs
are sheer and hooved   like a sublime doe
and she is gorgeous,   graceful in that plunge,
exquisite as he has   not ever seen her.
Her descent ends as   She slips into depths
of water below, little   sound of bodies hitting.
Ripples, eddies pinch up   into pageant of flaring
colour, menacing electric   crackles as competing spirits
are torn asunder. Spirit   of darkness throbs bruise
colours into nearby water.   Beneath neon shifts of
bodiless spirit, Piper glimpses   a stretch of immense tail,
claws likely. Spirit struggles   in lake water, climbs
one wave falls on   the next. Until a flash,
a large creature breaching   then calm, spirit gone.
He sees, but does   hear a form surface
near shore. For deck   its shadow slips ashore.
Out of this night,   a creature was birthed
to unfamiliar land,   and darkness leashed.
Piper descends the   Pelee Islander II's
stairwells and through   still humming belly.

They surge to him   as he stumbles down
the ramp from ferry   to concrete road top,
jaundice lights above   fuzzy in night air
and Piper enters with   strut that proclaims
both his exhaustion   and shared elation.
A path opens through   the islanders, Dustin pads
in, face cleansed of   make-up, covered up
in old housecoat   the handsome chiseled
mug of a man   returned, mangled with
joyous embrace from   ecstatic Roddy Piper.
He recalls past   months as memory not
his life lived, dreams   left vivid for life.

He asks of this   Ahtuhxkwe one.
Piper replies simple   that "She's a real looker,
not much of a talker,   let's hope a swimmer."

Ambrose confirms   with Piper ahtuwok are
fine swimmers, ancient   ones arrived at Middle
Island to begin anew   their ancestral patrols.
These waters, named for   Ahtukawenik nation,
Waabiishkiigo, Sea   of Neutrals, welcomes
cleansed manëtu.   reconciliation with
another lost relation.   This battle of light
and dark, through violence   has delivered a return.
Bridge top ferry lights   burn gold against sky,
empty like a reignited   lighthouse, the beacon
to be seen from   afar, fire reignited.

Òwiye

Thakwihëlake, sun   reflects path on water.
The Islander ferry calls   out departure, Carrianne
and Kelly offer medicine   pouch, island essence carried
with them, protection   to Piper and Dustin as
they have left protection   for them, Ahtuhxkwe
has been spotted at   shore near Vin Villa,
with dark medicine clear,   she dutifully minds after
her charge, island women   and children. Piper thanks
them with signed glossy   portraits, sincere wishes
to return for pheasant   hunts, beaches patrols, quiet.

The two ilaok drive   off in Piper's truck,
into the luminous   belly of the Islander.
Ivan, Kelly, Guido,   Ambrose, Carrianne.
together they all   look on as ramp
locks away. They are   left again, unaided
upon their ancestral land,   visitors carried away
across the waters that   divide worlds, and in
the ferry's wake is   a bejeweled way across
a fickle inland sea.   opens, then fills back
to the smooth peel   of water, spreads clear
the pathways a ferry   and people cut the lake.
The Pelee Islander swings,   her slow pinwheel
of radar and glides   into the night of
far off tv waves,   distant freighters flickers,
sails on towards   Kingsville's shore lights.
Those assembled at   dockside move away,
along the shore to   the south, èlikhatink
of trailer and poplars   at their assembly point,
where water, earth, sky   make stellar reception
from the scramble of   Toledo television signals.

They have gathered again,   as grand councils must,
in the shed behind   the shell of the old
Casino at the island's   edge. Electric carnival
burns to life, sky   and lake reflect each
perfect gyration. Above   opànalànkok peers
past clearing patches of   clouds, lingers into light

gaze upon trees, grass   tickled with sweet dew.
High above the wind   hisses about passages,
marks out time as   movement, leaves ground
and waters to reflect.   Rock, soil, and grass
beneath him, alone here   his island, their island.
Ivan walks the depth   of the lot, detours
through poplar stand as   he approaches trailer
he hears the crowd   of a Detroit cage match,
all frenetic joy at   spectacle. Ivan joins
them at the service,   alànkòk shines above all.

GLOSSARY OF TERMS

The following terms come primarily from the Unami Dialect of the Lenape language. Their inclusion in the work is a critical aspect of decolonization as it re-inserts this language, its unique cultural connections and connotations, and its sound back into a public usage.

achimëwakàn – story; anecdote; tale.

ahinu – great man; dignitary; business

Ahkonachimu – He who makes long speeches; refers to John Prince (1796-1870) Settler lawyer/politician. Led an attack that repelled American invaders to Pelee Island during the cross-border skirmishes of the 1830s.

ahtu/ahtuwok – deer (singular)/deer (plural)

ahtuhwixèkën – deer hair

Ahtuhxkwe – Deer Woman; a mythic spirit creature across multiple First Nations. They exist to punish men that harm women or children and hunt them after they do.

Ahtukawenik – Neutral Nation; People of the Deer (literal); Dominate pre-Beaver War nation that were the primary land treaty holders for the land along Lake Erie's northern shore. Were displaced through regional wars prior to major settler arrival. Waabiishkeego Gchigami is the Three-Fires Peoples names for Lake Erie that honours their legacy.

alais – hunter

alànkòk – stars

alënte – part

amimiyòk – passenger pigeons (*ectopistes migratorius*)

ashuwixën – the winds cross; specifically, they come from different directions as before a storm

awènik – people

azaadi/azaadiwag – (western dialect, Ojibwe) poplar/cottonwood tree

chëlìlhwès – kingfisher (*megaceryle alcyon*)

chëmàmës/chëmàmsàk – rabbit/rabbits

chikënëmuk – wild turkeys (*meleagris gallopavo*)

chitaninu – strong man

chkënakw – blackbird

èlikhatink – encampment; a camp

gaagaagiishibag – (western dialect, Ojibwe) double-crested cormorant; phalacrocorax auritus

Gchi-Ojiig – from western Ojibwe dialect. The Great Fisher (cat) constellation. Known by settlers as the big dipper. This constellation marked the entry point to the afterlife. The animal is not indigenous to Lenapehoking and the author could not identify a Unami Lenape name for the creature.

ila(ok) – warrior(s)

kaòkche – black-crowned night herons (*nycticorax nycticorax*)

kawënshuwik – honey locust tree (*gleditsia triacanthos*)

kishux – sun; moon; month.

ktàpihëna – we are here (inclusive we)

kuhëmëna – Our Grandmother; the moon in its mythological/ spiritual sense in the Lenape worldview.

kuwehòki – pine forest country

Kwèn'shùkwënay – Refers to Mishipeshu, the underwater panther of traditional stories. Known rival to the thunder spirits and protector of copper. Literally a panther.

kwshatay – tobacco

manëtuwàk – spirit beings

màxkw/màxkok – bear/bears

mënatay – island

mëtèxkwe – woman medicine person

mèthìk – evil; sin

Mëxumsa Ehëliwsikakw – Grandfather of the West

mòchipwis – turkey buzzard (*cathartes aura*)

mpi – water

mpisun – medicine (in contemporary sense)

mùxula – canoes

namèsàk – fish(es), pl.

naxans – my older brother; cousin (as in a familiar appellation amongst fellow Indigenous men)

naxkùntëwakàn – treaty; agreement

nekanemën – He sees it.

Neolin – Neolin was a Lenape prophet from the village of Muskingum in the lands now occupied by the state of Ohio.

nikanixink – leader

nipën – summer

Nkuli Punkw – translation of famous wrestler Goldust into Unami Lenape. Of gold (nkuli) and ash, powder, or dust (punkw). Placed in traditional syntax.

nushèmakòk – willow trees

òkwsàk – foxes

opànalànkok – morning stars

òpànke – next morning

opèksipu – White River; river that flows through current day central Indiana. Important and sacred river to Lenape/Delaware that lived there.

òsʰhakame – heaven (as in a vague spiritual or Christian sense. Not Kishelëmukònkunk, the dwelling place of Creator)

òwiye – later on

òxehëmu – moonlight

pishkok – common nighthawks (*chordeiles minor)*

piskapamùkòt – dark (atmosphere; as during a storm); dusky dark; the weather is cloudy and dark

pitay – foam on water (a term used to describe the hunger of settlers to consume/smother everything); it is foamy

pëmi – lard; animal fat; grease

pètapàn – dawn; morning is coming

pishkèk – dark; night.

piskewëni – night

pòkhakeho – to dig a grave.

punkwsàk – mosquitos.

sapëlehële/sasapëlehëlèk – lightning (singular)/ lightning (plural)

shukëli – sweet

tahkokën – fall (as in the season)

tëmakwe(yok) – beaver(s) (*castor canadensis*)

thakwihëlake – when the shadows are long; evening time

Tuwèhtuwe(yok) – Myaamiaki/Maumee/Miami person/peoples. Unami slang from these relations that we shared the territories of contemporary Indiana and Ohio with. Term is reference to Sandhill Cranes.

shukëli – sweet (compound portion of adjectival use)

Waabiishkiigo Gchigami – (nish) traditional name for what colonizers call Lake Erie. Translates roughly to "People of the Deer/Neutrals" and "Great Lake."

welhìk – that which is good

wetënteis – a scarlet tanager (*piranga olivacea*)

wicheochi – spouse; husband; wife

winakok – sassafras trees (*sassafras albidum*)

winkimakwsko – sweetgrass

wisawtayas – American goldfinch (*spinus tristus*)

wsike – sunset; the sun is setting

xaxakw – sycamore tree (*platanus occidentalis*)

xkuk – snake (generic term)

ACKNOWLEDGMENTS

The author would like to thank the Ontario Arts Council for their generous financial support of this work. Immeasurable depths of gratitude to the following magazines, anthologies, and editors for their support of my work on this project.

"Measurements" *Grain*, 49.1

"Dull Thuds over Waabiishkiigo Gchigami" *Sweet Water: Poems for the Watersheds* (Caitlin Press, 2020)

"Waabiishkiigo Gchigami Stills Herself in the Presence of the Pelee Islander II" *Rewilding: Poems for the Environment* (Flexible Press, 2020)

"Kwen'shukwenay Dwell Beneath" *Fiddlehead*, Winter 2020.

"Swallows Run Frantic at Water's Edge" *Watch Your Head*, November 2019.

"Sparks that Shall Not Ignite" *Great Lakes Review*, Winter 2023.

"Pishkok Perform Sunset Ceremony Feast" *Malahat Review*, Issue 222, Spring 2023.

"Our Slow Decomposition in the Reflection of Perry's Victory Monument Near the Shore of Middle Bass Island" *Malahat Review*, Issue 222, Spring 2023.

"Collecting Tipi Poles from the Pelee Island Transportation Company" *Malahat Review*, Issue 222, Spring 2023.

"Ghosts of Cranes" *Malahat Review*, Issue 222, Spring 2023.

ABOUT THE AUTHOR

D.A. Lockhart is the author of multiple collections of poetry
and short fiction. His work has been shortlisted for the
Raymond Souster Award, Indiana Author's Awards, First
Nations Communities READ Award, and has been a finalist
for the ReLit Award. His work has appeared widely throughout
Turtle Island including, *The Malahat Review*, *Grain*, *CV2*,
TriQuarterly, *The Fiddlehead*, *ARC Poetry Magazine*, *Best
Canadian Poetry*, *Best New Poetry from the Midwest*, and *Belt*.
Along the way his work has garnered numerous Pushcart Prize
nominations, National Magazine Award nominations, and
Best of the Net nominations. He is a graduate of the Indiana
University – Bloomington MFA in Creative Writing program
where he held a Neal-Marshall Graduate Fellowship in
Creative Writing. He is pùkuwànkoamimëns of the Moravian
of the Thames First Nation. Lockhart currently resides at
Waawiiyaatanong and Pelee Island where he is the publisher
at Urban Farmhouse Press.